C0 BEF 060

GATHERING *of* WANDERERS

"We sail over a vast expanse, ever uncertain,
ever adrift, carried to and fro."

 Pascal

"Great works are often born on a street-corner
or in a restaurant's revolving door."

 Camus

"All actual life is encounter."

 Buber

GATHERING
of WANDERERS

POEMS BY
WILLIAM HOLLIS

with photographs by ANDREA BALDECK

William Hollis

*For Tim, who will
get there!*

*Bill
15 May 09*

HAWKHURST BOOKS

Poems Copyright © 2008 by William Hollis

Photographs Copyright © 2008 by Andrea Baldeck

ISBN 978-0-9748304-3-8

Hawkhurst Books, 6122 Butler Pike, Blue Bell, PA 19422

www.williamhollis.com

There have been many islands
and encounters with many wonderful people
and while this collection is dedicated to all of them
(well, most of them)
it is particularly noted here as a tribute for
WYNNE AND GLENN CURRY
and the wanderers of Vieques.

CONTENTS

POEMS FOR YOU

1

When I was younger I would send friends a copy
of something that had been written at another time,
a postscript to show where I had been hanging out;
but gradually I find that as I write for you, or even
that other guy down at the end of the bar,
I try to turn words your way with rhythms of verse
and that curious twist that might avoid
the loneliness of a day at the top of the house
or out here in the open bohio where afternoons
drift in a blustery mesh from sea or jungle
and intrude on either the opera that buzzes badly
or these words that might make you lift an eyebrow
and chuckle and decide I'm still a bit crazy,
which is just as well when one becomes this old.

2

See, I was just going to drop you a note describing
a gradual explosion of interrelations on this island,
when something else starts happening to words
and the form they take almost by chance, even as
I am simply trying to describe a quick trip to town
to fill the jeep with gas, for there's often none
on the island and there was this morning, so we left
after early coffee, found it, ran into a new friend,
who is also a photographer and an old hippie
who still loves poetry and read one of my poems
at a recent party, beautifully enough to bring sighs
and a tear or two from guests, with gesture
and inflection we used among old piles of books
where we would lean and chant our poems.

3

But having discovered a form for these notes,
I'm stuck, wondering if I can describe the moment
we ran into a museum designer looking
for pawpaw at the old truck of the produce dealer,
even as it's ripening on trees among brush
in the dry gulch behind the truck, and she invites us
to come along and see the house she told us
about at a recent dinner when we first met,
as it's often the first time, though we think
we've seen everyone there is to see on the island,
at least of those who have intruded, returned,
and ended building retreats among hills
that stretch above the chaos of the world
and lift us toward clarity of moonlight and stars.

4

I want to write notes about a bit of liturgy found
on an old tatter, the sort of thing that begins nowhere,
goes nowhere, is translated with many parentheses
and left to be argued with, or about a few words
from a call in the middle of the night, something
more than a randy stallion smelling possibilities,
something we wake to and wonder where it went,
what it was or might have been, an echo from Verdi,
a set of notes that challenged Bach to find his way
even through back ways where feral dogs
dart at night and might not make it, might end
splattered on the road, subject matter for a hungry
photographer or for a raptor up and circling
at first light for a scattering of night victims.

5

Ah, my friend, don't get me wrong: every you
is you, the one I write to, the one I write for,
the one whose voice echoes in my head, has echoed
for so many years I no longer remember just when
or where it might have been I first heard
the tiff in the tone you drop at improvisations
that fail to tie one back to the basic line
that finds its way across a sheet of paper, a light
that cuts darkness from disparities that drive us
to the edge, you know, right here where you said
we'd never be — not here where those old guys
went or should have gone, but not us,
for we are wrapped in power of work, you said,
that's all we need to escape a curse that echoes.

6

There are marvelous singers on the Met broadcast
this afternoon who just now rise to the last fall,
carrying these poems with them after many hours
and now cheers as the audience confirms its acceptance
in a flutter of sound waves that make me wonder
if what I heard could have been so good, if what
I write beclouds my ears and keeps me from hearing
what I thought I heard; and now more cheers, many,
for base or tenor, soprano or mezzo I cannot tell —
cheers, if only for getting it finished, dropping us
over the side of the terrace, back into the jungle
and rushing growth of whatever will keep going
in a world where so little is worth it, where most
is forced, and only occasionally will words appease.

BESIDE THE WATERS

We live with passion above the surface of the sea
on an outcrop of rock from where we watch
barracuda, larger than imagined, break surface
and inevitable glitter of light disappear
as sun sinks with a final flash of green.

And if not there, we sit in an open window
above The Grand Canal and watch fantasy boats
dip and roll with harried tourists in a rush
to get to another landing, another dock where time
won't remind them that it will soon be over.

Or again we settle on the brushy edge of a bay
where raptors rest as sunset calls from the west
and we walk to the dock to see a scurry of crabs
that sink at our approach and watch remnants
of life stir the surface of quiet possibilities.

2

Here we are again on a hill above a field
watching a moon laugh as time passes,
hoping that our small pond of calm
will fill with artificial stirrings of swans
that remind us there has to be that water.

There has to be that surface to mystery
that sends reflected light across the afternoon
and says, just look below, for whatever
you see is what you've never seen;
just keep it there, don't let it drift away.

It's always there, below a surface that glitters,
that sweeps that way or this in a few hours
with rhythms like a beating of the heart.
If we'll just listen as we watch, we'll hear
things for which we've never found the words.

RHYTHM AND BOUNCE

1

I've lost the rhythm, lost a sense of movement
that carries that kid across the room from bar
or kitchen, a tray of salads, a couple of beers
at balance, one hip up, a shoulder down,
breasts that bounce in time to music. "A friend's
music," she says and bounces to greet another.

I wonder if her grandmother moved that way
and let her body flow toward a kid like me.
I lift my bottle, the beer lies still, with no
response to my body, no movement of life, just flat
as I must have seemed to all those pretty girls
when I was young and wanted to bounce to a beat

as if iambic notes could be the savior
and carry me with grace into the kitchen.

2

I've lost the rhythm..., never had the bounce...,
and fell from my mother's womb with a thud...,
but wonder now if tears of hunger or pain
echoed through the house with howling dogs
in imitation of those falling trochees
from old man Lear with his "Never, never, never."

I've dropped good bottles of a bright, young wine
and dropped my body across the bloody floor,
and found, as I watch young ones move around
the room, that I can rise, though no one sees,
and move to the rich dance of life, from there
to here with a stiffness in these ancient joints

as they ascend or descend the scales of Bach
and twist and counter twist until resolved.

BEADING A VERBAL BIKINI

She moves from here to there around her truck
like a word unsure of where it might set down;
she doesn't see the eyes that watch her path
and wonder where she'll find the words to throw
around and make a bench to spread her gems.

She's thin, not sure if she's a noun or verb,
perhaps the latter since she doesn't know
what's moving her from where to where in time;
she's here without a need for modifiers,
without a need for the little that she wears.

There are certain words, when I can find them
that help me see her with her aging skin
still tight, though worn with overuse and hope
that tweaks will put it right again, for polishing
with beaded words will never be enough.

But if one stops to look at jewelry she makes,
she seems to fall in place between a high
and my exhausted reach to find a gem
that might redeem the time I've hurried past
while looking for a sentence to make her real.

A necklace can be that way, a sentence too,
for a few of the lucky ones whose body holds
as structure for their words, as setting for
a memory of pacing restless verbs
that seem unable to pause, to find their phrase.

She comes and goes, our friend reminds us often,
she's here and there and then she disappears;
and we are left to wonder if she will ever
find a sentence that takes her to the point,
a pause, a place where she can sigh, "It's done."

LOSS OF NAMES

It's just a matter of remembering names;
you know, that beautiful woman we met at the door,
the one with flame in her hair and a touch of sweat
on her brow? And was it he, lurking as in
a lair, waiting, seeming to wait for prey,
perhaps the woman who turned away as he leapt?
What were their names, the ones that slipped away?

If I could find her name, or his, in the air
that blows against my face and spares the sweat,
I'd think that maybe I was young enough
to try again to wrap my tongue around
the possibilities I always felt
were waiting here, right here in the empty air
above the heads in an overly-crowded room.

Do I forget the names because I've found
a hint of drama in their eyes, like she
whose nails struck fire from bright stones
she wore? I sat with a blonde the other day
and watched her anger gather like flies deep
within her eyes; and then she left
and I am left to wonder what's the tale.

The names are gone, the stories too, but words
will linger here, fall down the page and find
a form to say you know you're wrong, that's all;
you've got the rage to pull them into shape
someone else might recognize and share.
Who cares what the name might be? It's part of you,
it's part of what you've always been; that's all.

MORNING AFTER

1

She pulls a chair close between us and whispers
something I can not hear, she can not say;
she does not look at us, but seems to stare
at scattered crumbs across a messy table.

She says, "I threw him out last night, just out,"
and looks around to see if someone needs
a refill, if someone is waiting for a bill.
"It's been coming for a very long time."

She sighs and adds, "I've warned him before, over
and over; and now I'll have to care for his mother."
Her shoulder drops a little more just for
a moment, just a moment, and then she rises.

I reach to touch her arm as she pushes her chair
and gathers up the cups, saying, "You'll want
another before you go — fresh cup of coffee."
And then she leaves with a limp of silence.

2

The morning after..., "It's always the morning after,"
she says, pulling a chair back to our table
where she may cry or laugh as I watch the corner
of her eye, the space between her teeth.

"He left," she says again. "I threw him out
and he left, just left; and here I am, the morning
after a night that I had waited for,
a long night during which I did not sleep."

3

We've watched her age and wondered if we
would end on the same limb that dangles above
heavy waters of the bay; but that
was a tree that fell in a heavy storm last year.

It happens here: a tree will take its shape
with the approval of the neighborhood
until suddenly it's over with, that's all;
the morning after is another world.

I often reach for what else she might
have said if someone from another table
had not called to ask for a refill of his mug,
and she is up as always to serve with a smile.

Perhaps today, on the morning after, she'll smile
and maybe even laugh a bit when she
remembers that she'll go home at 3, alone,
to an empty bed propped against a wall.

TROPICAL WANDERERS

I

Colancos are a breed of wanderers, a strange group
who live on tropic islands, famous for sexual games
with psychoanalytic patients, or who, as young men,
run local porno trades and give away family treasures
because they have no money to care for them,

especially in the tropics, and go by strange names
never heard in Boston, and gather on Tuesday nights
for dinner, each paying his own way and challenging others
to finish a bottle more quickly, so 2 or 3, dying
from cancer, can fly to Atlanta for regular treatment,

and one steals a plane so he can fly to see his companion —
weirdos totally free from constraints of modern life,
free from political, religious, intellectual, or emotional ties;
readers whose books have rotted in tropic air,
parents who have freed themselves from judgment

by grown children, anxious ones who write bad books
and build large houses to rent out in order to survive
and end up living in a shack but are still spoken of
in bars as living in those mansions above secret coves
on the sunny, south coast of an island that protects them.

2

Those are the colancos, a bit of jingoism that makes
no sense; but there are others, ignored by colancos,
never invited to Tuesday-night dinners, because...,
well, I don't know why, but probably because
they do a little work, like that beautiful woman who,

once free of her Vermont hill family, became a massage
therapist, very good and very sexy, who wears little
and stands high on one's body, while rushing to finish
so she can slip home to her strange, non-working husband
with whom she shares odds and ends of lovers,

3 or 5 in bed at a time, we're told — yes, most of them
work like a wonderful woman from Wisconsin who cleans
houses after escaping the cold of her family and that state,
and is another dying of cancer, but not before she gives
a party for us and non-colancos where a young doctor,

who now pulls bottles from ice buckets instead of babies
from female bodies, reads, in a lilting voice, several poems
to the group, as does a marvellous, drunken wife of an ex-doc
from south Georgia, who reads without stumbling, finishes
and collapses for the rest of the evening as a retired French

whore who ran a pole-dancing club in London threatens
to climb the balcony over a rock cliff where waves pound —
she will show us how to strip, how it should really be done,
she says, until her companion, once a famous photographer,
pulls her back from certain death, gives her another bottle

to drink from, and someone else, a lovely aging woman
who has, somehow, survived down there for 40 years
without money, picks up another book that someone
has taken from our house and reads another poem
as tears roll from her eyes, from mine, from all eyes.

3

And there are others, removed from the rest of us,
living high on mountains in modern houses among large
volcanic rocks, who occasionally want checks for favorite
charities and invite us for dinner and polite chatter
between a former head of a west-coast library of rare books

and a woman whose family had money for hundreds of years,
and a retired architect who'd rather paint large paintings
for which he'll build another room on the edge of the sky
and an old lady who, even on a small island, has a house
above the harbor and a country house where the island

drifts into the Caribbean through mangrove swamps;
and there's a lovely woman who tells art museums how
to run more efficiently, even though she can barely
connect beginning, middle, and conclusion of a sentence
in one fence line, and her husband who ran a museum

for the government, which drives him, of course,
to restless behavior and disappearance for a few days,
until someone will say, "Oh, by the way, he's back;
and there's something dark in the fellow's eye." There is.
It's the shadow where wanderers try to survive.

TALKING AT THE DINER

As we talk of those diseases that might
strangle breath and leave us turning blue,
I suddenly hear a woman trying her best
to sound far younger than her edgy voice
that with a sigh touches my ear and pulls me
from attention to a friend: "It is as if
we've never even been married...," she says
and sighs away the words, "I'm never there...."

My friend, who moves through bumpy times,
must have assumed that I was making notes
on his account, for he pauses when I push
a note across the table, gathering coffee stains
to smear words I've just written, words
I hear, the ones I've just jotted down,
the ones I don't really understand.
"I don't understand," he says and looks up.

I gesture behind me, for that's the way I do it:
I hear her voice that may have nothing to do
with illness as he and I discuss it; and her words
point at the larger illnesses of the world
we've watched for so many years — the failure
of people to get together, until we find
there comes a time for us to look about
and wonder if we're even here at all.

And are we only here between plates
a kind but toothless waitress delivers, smiling,
knowing that we are talking of the death
that faces each of us, sooner or later?
We might as well explore possibilities,
as maybe she is doing, not in old age,
but as years begin to crowd us out
and leave us with a kind waitress at the diner.

GATHERING OF WANDERERS
In 50 Sonnets

I

A full moon rises slowly from a hill
beyond a harbor where sails are furled.
It gains rich color as the sun sets
behind us and the world goes dark

except for a shimmer of moon on water
here at our feet or way out there
where sails have disappeared and dark
comforts a beleaguered craft at rest

after windy weeks at sea, after toiling
for anchorage, after a bluster of time
that drives us into these quiet harbors,
these places where we can call it quits

with politics and the greed of war
flooded by a moon now overhead.

2

A bottle of champagne is handed to each
of us, with a straw and careful instructions
for proper toasts and songs. Not an indulgence
I've made in fifty years; but, after all,

it is, for them, a gesture of acceptance,
a sharing of their world, an invitation
to return. "You'll see," she says, and smiles,
"the stories are endless; you've hardly begun

to know what might be known." Everyone laughs
and finishes a bottle. Our hostess nods,
salutes the sea and leads us to table,
our cheeks flushed with colors of merlot.

"Sit here," she says, "and I'll tell you a tale
to make him blush, though, frankly, he never has."

3

She's never known, has never had to know;
the world had cut her free and left her on her own:
her father disappeared, her mother floundered
and she was left to wander on her own.

"I've never understood the Eves of the world,"
she says, laughing with a burst of innocence,
"accepting what he said, cowering in a bush;
at least she had the guts to cut the apple,

even if it meant they had to leave."
She sighs a sigh without judgment, without pain,
that in a moment leads to a snort of laughter
and stirs the dogs and sends a cat running.

"It's just myself," she says. "I can fly here or there
and be back at dark, just as owls come out."

4

"I'd never know," he says; "I'd fall asleep
just as a call would come to say a baby's
almost here." He pauses with a smile
and pours our wine. "And now," he says, "I pour

a drink and then I quit and go and sleep
or stroll Sun Bay at dawn and stretch and laugh
aloud and wonder how the others do it."
He seems an ordinary bartender until

we talk and find our paths have crossed, in spirit
at any rate, in trying to do our duty,
in trying to make the world a better place.
I watch him as he looks beyond the bar

to the sea and distant stretching of a world,
where real possibilities fade with the sun.

5

We sit at the far end of a bar and watch
a tall blonde arrive and leave with teetering
trays of dirty glasses or greasy nibbles.
She moves down the path, beneath palms, wavering

like an insecure model on a runway,
her hips to the left, her shoulders to the right,
her chin high, and no expression on her face.
But when did I ever see a fashion show?

I wonder. Perhaps she mimics a movie
with gestures calculated to swish a skirt,
attract attention, which seems not to happen.
She splashes a little wine when she places glasses

too far from our reach with no acknowledgement
and swings down the runway into the night.

6

There are tears in her eyes and rising doves
on rusty metal she paints; and when
her husband enters, she does not glance at him
but slips from the room like a timid kitten.

There's something gentle and damaged in her,
a passion that we respond to, want
to know, to share, but know we never can.
We bring a dove home that hangs beside

the desk where I write these lines and remember
her beauty and the deep sadness of her eyes
and wonder if she will be lifted by doves,
by the work she does, so beautifully that

now, within the greater sadness of the world,
I think of her and the light in which she works.

7

The only time she smiles is when he enters,
bringing her chilled vodka, a paper to sign,
a bowl of soup. He never smiles, though we soon
find ourselves smiling at his solemnity,

like that of a solemn cat who purrs down deep.
We want to hug him, to bring him a drink,
to prod for stories that are rising close
to the surface and twitch like a cat's whiskers.

Only later did someone say he is ill,
and then we notice his hand hesitate,
just a slight shifting of the weight of the world,
as he brings another bottle of wine,

before he sits and says softly, "We once talked,
you know, when shadows were following *you*."

8

She stretches and the rips in her shirt gape
and her skin glows with reflections of the sun
as she shrugs and possibilities fall
from her heart like hopes she had when she was young.

"It's all another world," she says; "I forget
the ways I had as a girl — decades..., you know
those passionate experiences of hope."
And now she swings her scythe across the grass

that springs everywhere from fields we thought
were just that possibility itself.
She throws her arms to the sky and cries aloud
and laughs and draws defiance for her years.

I smile and shrug and stretch these aging bones:
while *her* possibilities will still continue.

9

He sends a message that he's not coming,
obligations tie him to some other world,
over there, wherever; other islands, he says,
like the one we are on, are always somewhere.

"I had to move on," he says. "It was over,
not there, perhaps not here. It was just a dead end."
We read the message, not quite believing it,
and wonder if his house is part of the deal,

a final retreat for him, for us, the end
of a voyage that has taken us around
the world and back again. We wonder if we
should write and insist that he come and visit

alone or with his new friend. There's still something,
we think, some reason for being here — or there.

10

She stands in the center of a room and surveys
a domain now hers, for awhile, hers alone,
and sees that we might need more wine, and comes
to offer something more, a little something

that just might please the palate if we wish,
and all we have to do is lift a finger
and nod in her direction, that's all we do,
and she will bring whatever might be wanted.

So it's not surprising when we find that she
has left it all, her husband, house, and kids,
a business that, she says, was doing well.
Whatever tears with which she held on tight

are gone; her eyes are dry and focused on
the moment until we pay the bill and leave.

11

Eight of them, with pleasant smiles, are at the door
asking if they can look around.
They smile and introduce themselves
as farmers from Lancaster who have, by chance,

found themselves on this strange island where
certainly the beaches are something special,
but there is a strangeness in the air, a whiff
of burning without smoke, a silence at night

that makes them glad they all came together.
They thank us for showing the house and leave.
From time to time we see them walking the sand
or gathered in chairs at the edge of the sea.

We never see them at a bar or café
and lose the card where they had written names.

12

We've seen her almost every day,
restlessly circling her battered jeep
or sitting at a bar with a plate of greens;
and if I speak, her eyes blink

and try to focus somewhere beyond
my ear as if trying to read an aura.
Her dreadlocks seem to be failing;
and when she walks, her red bikini

is the only thing that doesn't slip;
she walks as if pulled by gravity
into a world of aging sex and dreams.
"It's just *exaggerated lumbar lordosis*,"

my wife murmurs in mild distraction
as we watch the aging belly circle.

13

She's large like a Viking, she says, and tall,
vigorous like a Scot. Her husband, she says,
is from New York, a psychiatrist, she says,
who limps about refilling drinks and waiting,

seeming to wait for something new to come
across hills that rise from the sea. He nods
and gestures toward the garden as she rises, says
that it is time to leave, her sons are waiting.

"You must come again," she says with a grand sweep
of arms and toss of golden hair; her husband
will be so pleased, she says, as he almost smiles,
a first time, and holds my hand with a caress

and says that I must see his gardens, next time,
special gardens, he says, full of surprises.

14

Her skin, like leather, as will happen when
you mess with fire, is sleek and polished by
sweet oils of avocado. She drips with green,
a daemon made by children on a dare.

Who knows how old she is or when it was
she danced with fire and twirled a burning stake
and chanted to the wind, to passing raptors
who circle high and, in her updraft, higher?

She landed here because.... Well, because
she felt few places left would tolerate
the energy with which she faced the world,
the freedom she consumed — demands she made

by lifting her eyes, by seeing as only she
could see by looking, opening her eyes to see.

15

He doesn't return, he says, but stays right here
on a hill overlooking a stretching sea,
where distant islands catch the sun before dark
and a gay crowd gathers at dusk for drinking

and elegant casting of casual invitations.
"He's a grandfather," she tells us, "but still prowls;
we threw him out last week when he had a fight
over a cook who had just come from Boston

and is pretty and searching but turned him down."
We ask him why he never returns to Maine,
but he laughs and signals for another drink
and introduces us to his plump companion

who has nothing to say but smiles politely.
"That's the way it is," she says when they are gone.

16

For a day or two, wild horses come
and feed in the lower field, neigh,
perhaps mate or simply dance
in ways they can when free of reins;

and then they're gone, nowhere seen,
wandering to a more distant valley
or dying in arroyos as others move on,
form new alliances, flourish and die.

But for this day or two, we watch
and laugh in expectation as a young one
rears and neighs as if for the first time
and the others, youngsters themselves,

pull back and seem to wonder what's up
in a dance step to try before death.

17

The horses seem contented in a way
those guys who hang around The Green Store
can never be. It rains, the grass is fresh,
their piles of shit are rich enough to use

in pots of herbs; the guys who drink all day
seem constipated, straining at relief,
anything to let memories slip away.
The horses just below me in the field

occasionally lash out to see who's boss;
the guys have tired of that, of everything,
except another beer, another tale
about the jeep that burnt, the other guys

who didn't make it back, who suddenly
were gone like silent horses who disappear.

18

He is thin and tan and old and still looks good
as he sips on his gin and tells another tale
of friends we've had in common, though we've not met
until now, here on this island of homeless

wanderers, casual passers-by, loners
looking for a moment that will finally
explain it all, a moment when one can say
"Of course, that's it! Yes, that's what it's all about."

Lovely, he says, that we should know so many:
a lover he had at school, but had not seen
in decades, with whom we'd recently shared drinks;
a surgeon whose notorious escapades

can still give rise to a laugh that now we share
as we sit on a terrace above the sea.

19

She smiles and plays the perfect host, gives a hug,
serves a plate of cheese, and says, "I'm fine," grimly,
"just fine." Her eyebrows flicker as she consumes
her flesh in a futile effort to control

a faltering world; so, thrusting cheese, she smiles.
We'd known of each other in another life
but never met, not even to remember names,
until the fog is swept away by rains

and then suddenly her mother's face appears.
"My god," I say, "your mother was the one who...."
"That's right," she says, "yes." "But were you there?" I say.
"Rarely," she says, eyebrows thin and flickering.

A history lingers in the air and a chill
rises from the sea as the terrace darkens.

20

A grey king bird poses on a dead branch
of a naked indian tree as the sun sets;
he poses, stretches, and then flies off, regal
and independent. "A very good sign," she says

and smiles and turns back to us and the sea,
though we know she sees it all, whatever it is,
a small lizard with circles on his skin
who slips down a banana leaf or a raptor

who circles above a distant island, beyond
anything I can see. And who knows
what she has seen in me or a passing stranger:
a mutilation of fears or aging hope?

Perhaps that's why she keeps a bed that's narrow,
protection from the dreams of someone else.

21

We never hear his name; but over breakfast,
we watch him pour a splash of brandy in tea
brewed black before he walks or rather trips
about the village with a gnarled, handsome cane

that Lona gave him after he was crushed.
He is said to wish that he had not survived
to sell those damned t-shirts to a few tourists
who quickly take a ferry back to San Juan.

Later in the day, we'll pass an open door
of a bar and he'll be one of only three
sitting in silence, drinking, brooding perhaps.
Wounds can be inside or out, I say to myself,

as Andrea pauses to photograph the pain
drifting from an open door in silent smoke.

22

He wants to come, wants to bring his wife;
after all, his son had brought the grandsons here,
scrubbed and neat and well behaved. They loved
the bay, tolerated food, and were not at all,

they said, comfortable with people
who served them at a hotel we never saw.
We ask him please to wait for another time;
we can't just say he'd never like it here,

though it is true he wanders more than we,
sticks flags in all the countries of the world.
"We'll see them all," he says, "four or five a year.
All those empty places we'll see, while you slip

away and settle down in a place with no
attractions." Just the people, I think, just them.

23

She only comes down between books, to see him,
to tell him how much she loves him, to give hugs
and greetings to the islanders; but she'll leave
quickly, back to other lovers, editors,

a house to replace the one that washed away.
It is, we tell each other, material
for stories she publishes on schedule, each year
another tale that echoes all the others

and keeps bored retirees amused with tears
and laughter. Elegant clothes hang from bony
shoulders, flap on the terrace like silk flags;
when we exchange hugs, she clings with desperate

urgency, pushes her body close, and seems
to whisper a need, a need to whisper close.

24

His father is Irish, his mother local,
and he swings across the island with great loads,
striding dark with blue eyes and blonde hair,
a smile always on his face. He has fought the navy

and won, finally, after fatalities
the larger world ignored; and, now, a father,
he runs a small café and sells plots of land
to wanderers who think they might stay awhile.

He and his boys and sometimes his wife live
in two rooms perched above the sea with dogs
and three wild horses that wander across hills,
free of ropes, only ridden on holidays.

His boys will go off to school, he says, to find
a life he seems to feel has passed him by.

25

She throws her arms high and open in welcome,
her hair falls back as if she would sing, as once,
a time ago, she sang in the dark clubs
of San Juan. She stands on a balcony above a yard

of old cars, plastic bags at which dogs sniff,
and a refrigerator that will work, she says,
if they can ever plug it in — and with
grand gestures invites us, please, to climb the steps.

This woman who had sold good times to tourists,
until she ended up in jail for protesting
prolonged naval bombing of her home,
leads us, with a limp and obvious pain,

into a high cluttered room where she offers
wine or tea, a bit of cheese, a bowl of grapes.

26

"He gave me this," he says of a small twisted cross.
"It helps me through gutters and up hills," he says
and rubs and twists until it's bright with sweat
and looks a little like his own worn life,

one a priest might have to carry to the crest
of a mountain high above the sea and fence
with rusted razor coils to keep the others out.
I think he winks, though it may be a tick

in memory of things he wrote, back when
he could still fight a war of retribution;
it's what he came here for and had his children,
to carry on the fight. His body has shrunk

and there's a tremor in his voice. "Just once,"
he says, "I'd like to have the last word. Just once."

27

Somewhere along a road we've never known,
she'll suddenly say, "Here, stop here. That tree,
that stone, that barn.... It's what I'm looking for."
And with an eagerness far younger than

her years, she'll scramble from the jeep with eyes
already turned and searching for tones
and rhythms of a world long since abandoned,
at least in this field beside a rutted back road.

I find a bit of shade, a breeze, and pull
a crumbling notebook from my pocket, a pen,
and hope I'll find a rhythm for the day,
a rhythm for the restless life we lead;

though after a phrase or two, I glance across
the field in panic that she might slip away.

28

"We are," he says, "on the border of nothing.
Look there," he says, gesturing across the bar
to the sea, darkening even as we speak,
"there's nothing more to see except what is here."

An assistant slips in to say that a friend
has just arrived, is asking if he is still
alive, available for a small favor.
He shrugs and excuses himself for a moment.

We watch him leave, watch the waitresses relax,
order another glass of wine, wonder what,
if we could really do it, we would do now,
alone at a bar among many strangers.

"I'm back," he says, arriving back. "Would you like…,"
he pauses and laughs and orders another drink.

29

There's a subtle edge of pure brutality
that runs through the heart of this beautiful island;
you might not notice unless you looked into
the eyes of guys propped against rocks,

waiting restlessly, simply waiting
as sun grows hotter and wind blows harder,
whipping palm fronds in angry gestures
at nothing in particular, at just the day,

at a world that's left them drink they can't afford
and suspicious glances from tourists and cops;
if you try to call a greeting, give a lift
of the hand, their eyes drop to a bit of trash

blown among rocks by a gentle wind
when storms abate and sun colors the sky.

30

She insists we'll not be disappointed
with Mamalonga's dirty little café
and excellent omelets for mid-day breakfast.
We often return for potato pancakes

and an hour of listening to visitors
full of sad gossip and inner exhaustion.
And sometimes when there is no one else about
but this Irishman, a former journalist,

and his German wife, who does all the cooking,
we'll slip through a casual exchange of tales
that hold a lingering hint of something more.
She'll lift feet to an adjoining stool and sigh

as he hands her a ruffled newspaper
and a snort at what politicians have done.

31

The loveliest view from this island house
is from where I stand in the bath at the back
of the bedroom and look out across desk and bed,
out vast open doors, out over terrace and pool,

where dozens of hummingbirds dart and hover,
and look down hill over roosters that brag
and wild horses in heat that rear and neigh,
and out over a harbor where a few sails

catch brilliant sun, and on out to the horizon,
south further than I can imagine, though I know
what islands are unseen there or over there,
unseen from this loveliest view from the house

where I stand, several times each day, at the john
and piss, and have never enjoyed pissing so much.

32

I keep trying to read, to see what else
Annie Dillard might have to say; but no,
I am disturbed by the unreality of
a world that blows here with crows of roosters

and barking of feral dogs. I mean, where else
could I fall asleep dreaming of birds
flying across the bed and wake and find
their droppings on my pillow? It's unreal,

my daughters might have said at their father's tale.
No, I read far less than I write on islands,
trying to find a rhythm for the woman last night
whose story came out each time she passed the table:

parents who pushed, a husband who wanted too much;
and now she stares into the sun and laughs.

33

He sits at the bar and waits and looks around
and murmurs a comment to the keeper who nods.
He's eighty, it's said, but when he looks over rims
of his glasses and raises an eyebrow, I could swear

his eyes are seeing it all for the first time,
as if they are hungry to register a world, as if
it's new, always new, each face that enters,
a new story, an opening, a possibility.

We should acknowledge him, I say to the table,
and rise to approach the bar and take his hand,
and lean close to hear what he might say
after the years he has watched us come and go.

He lowers his glasses, blinks his deep blue eyes,
and murmurs, "I get a chill sittin' here at the bar."

34

"My father managed to survive the camps," she says,
chopping a little harder at a mango for drying.
"He never recovered, never found sanity
to know what I was all about as a kid."

Her salad with dry mangoes is a treat,
the best lunch, it's said, around the island,
when it's available, which isn't but once or twice
a week when she's sober, her knives sharpened,

her friend protecting her flank, aware of flares
that might occur when her knife flashes up
and down. It's clear that she's much loved now,
by that friend who keeps her voice low and cool,

knowing that it can end, that it can all end
for any of us, in a brief flare of a moment.

35

She holds three passports so she can come
and go as she wishes. "Off to Africa next,"
she says; "there's a hospital that needs my help,
in Angola." And she has a house in town,

just above the harbor, where she watches barges
arrive with truckloads of supplies and a large
family gathers for the winter. We meet
for lunch on the other side of the island

to explore questions about crazy humans
and to find where to buy a half-decent wine.
Andrea met her while touching the Mekong,
and it is she who said, "You just might like it" —

this island of wanderers that once seemed
only a target for a world's destruction.

36

He has come ashore to work on new gadgets
strangers have brought with them. He's the only
computer maven in the village; though blind,
or almost blind, he gives directions, waiting

to be told what the screen looks like now. It seems
precarious, but to work; at least we get
unimportant messages and respond
with something inane while he hovers to hear

if Andrea's portable is working now.
Then one night we see him at a crowded bar
in a flowered shirt as thin as his eyesight.
We watch as he stares into his drink, waiting

for something to happen, for an answer why
he'd come to a sunny shore he couldn't see.

37

I've begun to see how little we know of him;
I'm not even sure that he's a he, and sometimes
I think that she has found a perfect balance.
Perhaps that's what the world is all about

with her, with him, for even the name can slide
around without the twist of a gender's ring.
She's lived down here for a decade or maybe more,
doing odd jobs except when she disappears.

We like him, think there's more than a story inside,
something more than sex, that's tapping truth
in a way that makes us smile whenever we hug
and say hello-goodbye and know that soon,

perhaps, we'll have to sit and talk our way
in and out of the heart of where we are.

38

On this warm island smaller than most counties,
she owns two houses and has for many years,
though she only stays the winter months, alone.
Having seen the island from a yacht, passing

on another restless trip, she suddenly
decided to live here, to settle down, quit
a life that had driven her far beyond York.
She gives parties and tries to protect the dogs

that wander everywhere and die in gutters.
From the house in town, she points out wrecks
that line the harbor just below her garden,
a rich profusion with waterfall and pond.

She looks up at me and whispers, "It's not long,
not now," before we join others for a drink.

39

Is he the father of that little blonde boy
a young mother carries, looking glum
and heavy, not yet recovered from pains of birth
and shadows that linger in memory?

They drift apart as surf washes at sand,
covers feet and fails to clear away
tobacco smoke the father blows at the child.
The mother coughs, a wind blows harder, salt

and smoke and a nimbus frame the lovely child
as mother pulls him close and buries her face
in his hair while the back of her neck shakes
and father drifts further away from a smile

without even a shrug to show he doesn't care;
it was an accident — it happens, you know.

40

Later we discover Tropical Honey's,
with lunches full of grains and fruity salads.
She seems reluctant to share stories that flesh
out a meal and linger like fine aromas.

If not pushed too hard, if we just laugh, if we
share a real compliment one day, she'll throw
an extra hand of sesame seeds and sprouts
on sweet noodles the next time we're in for lunch.

The stories come, as they will with fine stroking:
escaping from a tsunami in Bali
thanks to the largesse of a handsome Frenchman,
never lingering long in any one place,

making sure the nuns threw her out of school
here in the same valley where I write these lines.

41

The sea changes daily, hourly. Right now,
if I just turn my head a bit to the right,
the sea slips up toward a pale blue sky
with no horizon, no line to say it's here,

this edge beyond which lies another world.
Last night, before the sun was fully gone,
the sea grew darker than a sky with no clouds,
grew dark and seemed to rise to a sharp edge

beyond which there was nothing, as sailors must
have feared sailing toward a vast unknown.
Perhaps clouds that rise like tumbling ruins
are hiding something we are afraid to know;

perhaps there was a world that disappeared
as we will disappear beyond the edge.

42

I thought the hedge remained the same — not really,
of course, for I've lived in gardens, know them well;
but for a month or so it seems to be
the same, a gentle lumping of green and yellow

along the wall. It isn't a garden we know
and soon we'll leave and others will come and admire;
and if the hedge changes, a hump flattens
and leaves enlarge or rot as worms take hold,

well, that is what others will see, a hedge
with green buds, no yellow, blocking a view
we see each morning as we wake and stretch
and rejoice we've found another world to know;

only we don't, we can't. Who can know a world
into which one slides before one's gone again?

43

She's surly and has been here since the birth
of a kid, serving drinks at night and breakfast
somewhere else, asleep at the helm, one might say,
except she is, someone said, protecting

that child with reluctance and a lack of grace.
"One can't complain," I say aloud. "It's just there,
a bump that itches while we wait for coffee."
Occasionally, I must admit, I'm less

than kind, impatient enough to feel better
by overtipping. At least it's for the child,
I say silently as she looks at the tip
and asks, without a smile, if I want change.

I wonder about her son, about her life,
if sunlight will ever rise within her heart.

44

They sit at table popping muscles and burp
and laugh without humor, except at farts;
they turn chairs to face a room where young
waitresses giggle and watch them rub their cocks

to make larger lumps in sleek cargo pants
they've worn all week. The oldest seems in charge,
his body's more at ease, a sag is hidden,
as gray pushes at a slick skull;

he seems to keep an eye on who drinks what
and with a quiet voice restores a calm
they seem unable to maintain as they talk
of California where they hope to find

more work: one speaks of another little film;
maybe, the older one says softly..., maybe.

45

"You'll never get to know the secrets," he says.
"I've tried. I've tried to know those who work
a winter here and then, returning to the Cape,
are gone, so not even dogs that they adopt

remember if they were really here or not.
And her, the one you like so much, was she here
last year? I couldn't say. Of course I was gone
myself; trying to move the shop." He has wine

and good cigars, or so I'm told, though only
gays who can afford the best will smoke them late
at one elegant bar, where whispering
is loud enough to overhear, and stories

are told to cover all the secrets at which
we can only guess, like reading a poem.

46

He's been on the island for fifty years or more,
running a bar or bordello here, a café
down by the wharf where special packages
arrived for his attention. Is he lurking

among the second-rate, defusing harmless
ones who wander before they trip and fall
into an arroyo, where bones wash out with those
of calves who never made it to an udder?

He still sits quietly as at an altar,
sizing up possibilities,
packages that just might yield a rise,
one final risk before the end. His large

unblinking eyes circle the room in silence,
slipping into a void that waits out there.

47

She snorts at the word 'possibilities'
and glances at my face. "It's all gone.
Whatever was there blew away with a war,
a hurricane, my husband with his trophy.

Don't talk to me about possibilities."
She looks back down at remnants of her lunch,
wilted greens, a smear of mustard, beer,
if any's left in the can she pushes around,

around and around, staring at the circle
of sweat she's left on the counter as Michael
smiles to himself and waits as he always seems
to do, watching a sadness in her eye,

in the eye of anyone who stops by, as he waits
to wash down the counter when the drama's done.

48

She's gone, it's said; but no one knows where.
She wouldn't return to the Cape, not after she slipped
from a bridge and lit the fire herself, and fled...
to Maine, perhaps, to remnants of a farm

she never really knew, because her father
lives on and leaves the place a mess, she said;
besides they've seen each other only once
in fifteen years; and that, she said, was shit.

Someone says he heard her say she'd go
alone, go further even than these islands
where she gathered feral dogs and fed
stray cats and lived alone on a brushy hill.

She's gone; that's all we know, and we wonder now
just what we may have missed and never knew.

49

It's time to leave — it happens to us all;
just as we think we've settled in and it's home,
at least a place that feels as home might feel,
as if we'd ever know, not those of us

who wander restless like feral dogs
and howl for a rising of the sun —
it's time to get a plane, to get on back
where gardens take forever before they're gone,

where friends grow old and fade like us, like all
of us who wander through fields wondering
what lies around a scattering of boulders
thrown from the earth by distant explosions

and left to mark these island hills with awe,
these hills where wanderers gather for the night.

50

"Will you come again?" she says. "Are you also
wandering?" She knows by now we listen in
on whatever can be heard or seen, the hints
of a quest, a hunger, or a hidden rage;

she's seen us at the bar pretending to read.
"There's one to watch," she says, "the blonde
in torn shorts. She's awfully good with a tray;
but wait awhile and she'll tell you of bodies

she prepared for burial and their cold flesh.
She's the best we have; she'll be here for a year
or two and then she'll wander on. Yes, she pays
her way and she's young enough to smile.

Her smiles are real. For now." She lifts her glass
and says, "Do come again; you can't escape us."

FINAL DARK GRAPES

We bring her a bowl of final dark grapes,
the last on the island it is said, as people gather
to watch a haze chill and then drop away
leaving dark heaviness, a jewel that one might eat.
It's a ritual, we are told, to watch last grapes
as they are consumed, delicately, one by one.

We hope she knows these grapes are for her,
waiting for her to reach, as she never will,
not again. But if she doesn't know, the rest of us do,
we are there for the afternoon with all the neighbors;
and at dusk, just as the sun begins to slip into the sea,
we pass a bowl for everyone to have at least one.

But for now, for an afternoon in the heat of the sun,
final dark grapes will grace the side of her bed;
and we'll stand around and talk of a last storm
and wonder if we'll avoid one in the coming season,
for there are seasons when all vines are crushed
while grapes are still small, green and hard.

But this has been a good year. She's lucky to go
when the harvest is good, grapes plump and dark
and neighbors still around, still there to come
and help us eat final dark grapes and share stories
she would have loved to hear, and would have told
as her own tale, a tale to make us laugh and cry.

HANDEL'S CRICKET

I never thought I'd want to kill a cricket;
but here we are, in an open house above
the sea and the moment Handel's flute comes on
a cricket begins to sing with a mating call
louder than three instruments together,
already tuned loud to accompany dinner.

I swallow sprouts, bang a fork against
a plate, shout imprecations to the air,
and wonder where in the high open room
the critter lurks, and threaten death —
though we know if I find the thing quivering
like a hummingbird who collapsed in a corner

of the bedroom that we cupped gently and took
to a bougainvillea where, after a short rest,
he rose, hovering, and fed with continued grace...,
well, if we find that damned cricket hovering,
we'll lift him to the dark terrace
and murmur inane terms of affection.

But right now, as I eat and, in a notebook
that lies near my glass, make these notes,
a fairly common dinner activity, as Andrea reads,
I have to admit with reluctance
that I hate the damned cricket and will, if I can,
smash him under an unhesitant palm.

ISLAND NOISES

To close a regular beat of a damned bell
by stuffing a sock in its rusted mouth
allows a rooster's bragging call
and the distant baying of feral dogs
to drift uphill and through a drafty room
where we almost sleep above the sea,
could be asleep but choose instead to be
awake, listening for an island's life.

And now, with half a day blown by,
a rooster struts and calls to let us know
the rutted path downhill will pass his brood
that's larger every day; and through the air,
a melody rises, note by graceful note,
until the sounds of Andrea's flute settle
like glittering light into a distant sea
that glimmers with a falling of the sun.

Palm fronds move like a dancer's skirt,
first this and then another way, here and there;
and a hundred more dancers cover hills
in costumes of various greens and tan,
swish in winds that never pause, that are here,
always up or down hills in more ways
than a mistress of the dance could plan,
in more ways than we can hear or see.

SUNRISE

Seventy years ago I saw the same brief burst
of sunrise color I saw this morning and said,
repeating as I did today, that I was glad
not to live in a city where such drama is impossible,
in an error I've often made, an anticipation
of darkness that will close me out, will leave me
wondering just what I should have seen coming.

Yet the tiny room I had as a student in Paris
was in the attic of a cheap hotel with one window
where occasionally, during darker times
of the year, colors of a sunrise would travel
across the ceiling and fall to my pillow
and pull me to that window from where I saw
the glowing dome of *l'Institute de Paris*.

And some decades ago, when a girlfriend
had a basement apartment on Lexington Avenue,
it just so happened that during one early morning
(or late night) quarrel, we paused to see a brilliant rise
of color reflected in yellows, reds, and oranges
on large windows of an apartment across the garden;
and it was just luck this did not save the relationship.

After my divorce I lived for ten lonely years
in two different apartments in Philly; for each
I searched for places that had windows
to west and to east — though I don't remember
any particularly morning when sun rose as a diva.
But during years when Andrea and I had a palazetto
on The Grand Canal in Venice, we watched sunsets

fall the length of the canal when there was clarity;
and, during the winter, light would flood a back alley
and fall through our garden into the bedroom,
like fire that lit the city on an early morning
when the opera house burnt and crumbled into ash.
Though now, as we age and settle down, our rooms
are often full of the fall of garden colors at dawn.

SCENES OF RETURN

A rainbow seems to push from a bank of clouds,
dark and slowly coming from beyond
a backdrop's fading line of disappearance.

We pause with a wanderer's arriving tread
and watch pale washes of color spread
as if attempting to script a call of welcome.

Pausing only to note the bougainvillea
still in bloom, I pull a pad and pen
to catch the hoped for, unexpected scene.

It may be jealous roosters and feral dogs
that welcome us with long and lingering calls,
but people from the wings are whom we wait for.

One has a mermaid's sigh from coastal Maine
or tears of a broken mother from the Cape
or sighs of someone who has just washed ashore.

They will arrive, I know, with hugs and tales
and, if we'll just stay quiet and listen, their pain
and laughter and tears will soon appear.

Her skin has coriaceous richness, dark
and smooth and sexy like Mongolian leather;
only her eyes betray a scar of battle.

We've watched her swing across a stage with trays;
we've sat with her at supper on the roof
and laughed at sad pretensions of the world.

We've hugged to bid goodbye and emailed notes
that never seem to carry what we feel,
just empty words, scripted to say we care.

Distracted by dancers for the night,
we find it hard to keep the beat and stumble,
pulling down sets and scattering laughter.

We'll have to generate a new production:
on Tuesday nights a dinner on the rocks,
on Friday mornings an attempt to find some gas.

Improvisation will be the key for Monday,
and maybe then we'll have a clue to the plot,
a sense that this is what it's all about.

So now we find a place for a red-headed dancer
who ran a cabaret as if the world
were on her pole and she the great north star.

Her son died and she ran away
and opened a casual tavern in the village;
and though all beat-up sets are now in storage,

she doesn't know whether she'll dance or speak.
Just give her time, she says, an act between
the scenes, a moment with the audience.

We keep on trying to make the image fit,
to put these words in a line across a screen
that's wide enough in spite of glaring lights.

Perhaps a scene with cookies on a sheet
of tin or Bach as he's pulled from digital keys
would give a feel for what it's all about.

Should I leave the curtains up on all of this?
Perhaps it seems a little much for the scene,
that extra glass that spoils the exit line.

The local revolutionaries, thin and pale
or fulsome and dark, drop by to welcome us
with hugs and bows and a touch of reticence.

Halfway between a life marked by pain
and dreams of islands in the sun, we exchange
words that hang like necklaces of ice.

And when we finish and take a final bow,
we'll go to Bananas for chicken and mango,
hoping we've said enough and not too much.

Perhaps a final scene is called for now
where gay roosters strut or aging girls
try one more move to a drummer's dying beat.

Local mobsters plan, between their beers,
attacks on the next bunch of tourists who try
to buy a bay and sink their island with glitz.

But the notebook's empty now, a pen lies tilted
against a mug, the coffee's cold,
the stage is almost empty..., the curtains close....

FAT BOSS

He rests his weight on a high stool and laughs.
Why not? He owns the joint; and the girls in black,
who place their order slips where he can see,
seem glad to be of use. They smile and duck
or turn away and frown before he shuffles
slips to see who might go first, who later.

I've sat and watched, a little hidden by rows
and piles of apparatus, and always wondered
if he ever frowned or always judged with laughter,
if this was what another generation
expected when they paused outside the gates —
laughter before an arrogant dismissal.

The girls in black have never lasted long,
a summer's break before they turn their backs
and leave the job to someone else still young
enough to giggle at the image of
a boss as large as this and full of laughs,
indifferent to the pain they may have felt.

LITURGY FOR THE ISLAND

I

Last night, we met more wanderers, this time proper ones,
     artists and curators from Toronto and Fishers Island
     who live here six months a year, raising funds to support
     educational programs for the young and full of careful
     tales that can be repeated without embarrassment.

The host house, the most spectacular on the island, is
     Wright-like poured concrete in five separate structures,
     perched on piles of volcanic rock, high on a mountain
     that overlooks Atlantic and Caribbean, with a pool
     that reaches space through illusion like the horizon itself.

We go tomorrow for a covered-dish supper with damaged
     forty-year-olds who give day and night to care for
     feral dogs and wild horses, and wait tables and clean
     rentals to pay for being here with or without a drunk
     companion who seems rarely available to help fix a toilet.

Today we wander back roads, which most are, to look for ruins
     of once-eager men from Milwaukee in casual bars or ruins
     of sugar plantations under growth of calabash, gliricidia,
     lime, and acacia as they flourish and rot at the same speed,
     leaving trash for mongoose who play mysterious games.

Tonight we'll throw chicken in a pot with fruit and root that
     haven't rotted and left squiggly worms on a gorgeous
     platter at the center of the table and add at the last moment
     a hand full of couscous, which may well have found
     its way here by a circuitous route through Africa.

After a long day's work yesterday, listening to *Onegin*
     from the Met, I now have pages of liturgy, with eleven
     days still to go, which could end up empty or full,
     since the only release from pain comes when words
     flow like old liturgy in double lines of Hebraic poetry.

2

Days go by and we see no one, though we hear workers
	curse and laugh on a castello being built by a Boston
	producer across the arroyo between us and the village;
	or someone will throw on brakes down in the village
	and curses will rise in morning air along the malecon.

From seven in the morning until four on most afternoons,
	even on Sundays, members of the family that owns
	the colmado, down where our dirt road hits the paved,
	will run concrete mixers, radios, and jokes in a house
	being built just over the bougainvillea hedge.

For most of that time I am at the computer, writing poems
	or letters that could be poems, or stretched on the bed,
	trying to relieve pain that makes it difficult to move,
	makes it impossible to do much of anything physical
	and puts my temper on edge, looking into the chasm.

Having just read, with admiration, Norris's *Cloister Walk*,
	I admire, even if not sympathetic to her faith, the elegance
	with which she speaks of liturgy as poetry and delight
	in rediscovery of Hebraic poetry I once taught and chanted,
	though never at ease with rhythms of the original.

Most evenings between six and seven, Andrea and I sit outside
	on uncomfortable tropic chairs, and watch light fade
	and constellations appear bright, except for a week
	before and after a full moon which pales even stars
	which for two weeks demark the sky and tell their tales.

As feral dogs bark, I decide to write this last letter for you
	with an arbitrary, accidental form for each sentence,
	hoping there will be material enough in some balance
	for prose to become verse as I discover once again
	that prose doesn't help except as liturgy chanted silently.

DINNER DRAMA

A dinner party should be applauded with cheers or boos —
or something appropriately in between: after all,
from the moment the curtain goes up until it's down
and the audience has departed, a dinner party is drama;
and no other piece of theatre, except experiments,
will replace actors with the audience while directors
and designers must enter as stars of all that happens —
while everyone must applaud themselves and bow.

Did our hostess applaud herself last night: "There, now,
that did go well!"? She should have, for it went well;
and the stage settings, a high terrace above the sea
and a dining room filled with a family's final treasures,
had taken years to achieve. Curtains parted with six
of the cast seated high on a rise as two latecomers enter
downstage around dramatic, volcanic stones which,
as lights dim, throw ominous shadows across the scene.

And is that calm Vassar actress really Meryl Streep?
And who is the bearded architect pretending to be old
and the wonderful comic who acts as baker of the cake...?
I understand they often steal an act or two in local shows.
And the other comic, whose eyes fail to hide amusement,
who purses his lips in an effort not to laugh...;
and the mysterious younger man whose distant look
speaks of dangers passed in process of less amiable plays...?

What a cast..., only surpassed by an actress who plays
director and reigns at table like a CEO seeing how far
she can let this program go before stepping in. Oh yes,
the two latecomers: she a lithe mystery, trying to survive
a shift from posing to performing, and he..., I mean,
after all..., when a visiting actor has to leave the stage
regularly, there's a problem. What is he really doing
when he leaves by a small door? What's hidden in his cane?

It's a mystery play where the victim is not present,
where crime, if there is one, is down below the stage
in one of those clusters of light that go on and off
as wind hits an expanse of glass and guests nod nervously
and the play ends, like so much of life, without a resolution
the stage used to demand, without a balance a dinner had;
but there was a lot of talk and talent enough to encourage
applaudable reappearances at other performances.

MALTESE DREAM

"It was another crazy dream,"
you say, "this time on Malta with Liesa,
the restless waitress from Rays, plopping
down coffee at the harbor that faces
the sea where they still wait for saviors
to arrive, to come sailing in
from the open sea with sharp laughter
and dull knives, at least in dreams."

"I suspect she'd enjoy such a place," I say;
"she's cared for everyone else. It's time
she wandered freely on the edge
of a cliff, waiting for the sun
to set, and suddenly see across
what seems an endless sea, though small,
just there as the sun disappears,
as a sail approaches, a cluster of sails."

"That's mine," you say; "not yours or hers;
that's my dream," you say. "You and Liesa
were there briefly while I looked about
for a way down through rocks to the surf,
until it was time to climb the mountain
that would take me home, over the crest
and down through green forests that flourish
only in the thickness of my own dreams."

"It's a place I know little about except
in dreams," I say, "dreaming of knights
until a sun rises from the sea
and leaves me wandering about the room
until you wake and we go to the diner."
"You wait," she says with a laugh; "Liesa
remembers that you splashed coffee
in the dream and forgot to leave a tip."

"Yes, you laughed at the idea of sails
approaching to remind us of something,
of something we said we had to remember."
We laugh with hope knights are real,
that we can find our way across
the cliff and down to welcome them
before the contradictions of day
have washed us out and away with tides.

GATHERING STORMS

My memory is full of islands and those
who wander and come to rest, for a while at rest,
here where a sea rolls in, around and on
to somewhere else where others wander

or come to rest, for a short while at rest
until these tides build up and winds blow in
and we gather in the harbor, waiting for something,
waiting for what we are not sure could be,

a party at the bar, a tide that rises faster
or winds that rise with echoes of other worlds,
laughter washed with tears, a falling palm,
one less to age and fall across the dock

as we gather close to tell tales breathlessly
like approaching storms and the wanderers we are.

UNMARKED GRAVE

The grave has been filled, dirt piled,
a family dispersed, our lunch served,
when, as we sit to eat, she cries, "Look,
"that gorgeous horse, one from a dream."

Alone and dark against the sky,
at the crest of a hill overlooking
a cemetery beyond a small bay,
he seems to watch the grave, just dirt,

no stone, no name to mark the plot;
and then we hear him neigh, a call,
an angry sound that crosses air,
falls from the cliff and survives surf,

an angry crushing fall of the sea,
a wind from the lungs of anxiety.
"Listen," she asks, forgetting lunch,
"is that anger or fear that drives him?"

He neighs again, mane and tail
lifted by wind, and then he leaps
to a full gallop, down the hill
to an edge of the cliff, where he stops,

wheels about and gallops twice
around the grave and back to the ridge
and pauses noble and free of reins,
as still as a horse cast in bronze.

We sigh and hold each other with chills
until, after a brief rear, he heads
at a greater gallop to the edge of the cliff
and down a path we had not seen,

down toward the sea and washed stones
and crushed shells, neighing until gone,
an operatic neighing that dies away,
dropping into an arroyo and gone,

leaving the cemetery to a thousand graves
and a clump of dirt for an old friend,
a boy with whom he'd climbed the hills
or a woman who brought him bits of bread.

We never see him again.
He isn't from the neighborhood
where we know by sight equine families
who wander, eating anything green

and leaving their piles of shit
for stately egrets to feed among.
He's another of the dream horses,
a horse flying from ancient Mongolia.

We'll be eating lunch in a fine place
and she'll suddenly lower her book,
reach out and touch my hand. "Remember,"
she'll say, "that gorgeous black stallion?"

and I'll say, "Like a dream horse," and sigh,
and we'll lean across the table and touch.
"I wonder," she'll say, "if they placed a stone
and carved a name above that grave."

BACH AND THE WIND

I

We step into wind tuned as high
and distant as clouds that gather
and break and sweep across the sea
from mountains rising gray and blue
over there beyond this windy terrace.

Behind me Bach, on a single cello,
struggles to give form to a crush of sea
that falls on ancient stones
slowly changing their shape as strings
give form to a bluster of wind.

2

The doors of the house rattle with wind
out of the east, a long journey
that pushes hard toward the sun,
as I sit and try to find rhythms for words
to place on paper the world we've found.

Isolated from what we've known, the island's
roar without rhythm leaves me
wondering if all that's left is prose.
It's hard to write with a heavy stink
drifting from dead ends of the world.

3

If great deserts of the East still blaze
with me or you or the other guy
falling dead because we lit fires
that blaze beyond our understanding,
it's harder to write or pluck strings.

I thought we had finally left the horror
with its heavy stink of flesh drifting
from cemeteries; I thought that here
we'd find tranquility, time to touch
with laughter and agony of years.

4

Is it anywhere? From a high hill
that overlooks the sea, an old man
waves a greeting we return with a smile.
He could be an ancient host, with tent,
a cup of tea, protection from storms.

He'd never know our Bach, our hearts;
but that wave beyond the cemetery
gives us a lift. We bend closer
to a speaker as the cello turns
to us in greetings that reassure.

PASSAGE OF A PELICAN

My book has fallen shut and slips to the floor;
I'm not asleep, just mesmerized by sea
and a pelican crossing, almost within touch,
right here, where I can reach and feel the air
that holds him on a steady course somewhere,
it seems, a million years without a pause.
I'm just a blur to him, if even that,
as he passes, leaves an empty undrawn line
between sea and sky and nothing else,
a wrinkled sea, a sky without a cloud.

The wind has blown the pages to a poem
about the rolling deserts of Central Asia,
the ones I wrote about when I was young,
the ones I've never seen except in dreams,
except when following from page to page
contorted passages and ancient routes
that seem as empty as an empty line
that cuts high into Tibetan hills
where bells echo tidal memories,
reminding us there's somewhere else.

I've not fallen asleep: the sea is here,
beyond the steady glide of pelicans,
beyond whatever it is I might have read
if the book had not fallen to my feet.
I sit and stare, glancing down at the book,
and am at one with rhythms of the sea
more complex than anything that I can say,
until I reach for pad and pen and kick
the book aside and start these lines
with a casual passage of a pelican.

WOUNDED GULL

The sea fell with a thump of heavy winds
as sand rose to scrape the unguarded face;
a gull tried to accept the wind, was buffeted
sideways across a dune in a moment of panic —
as if that was I, in a small windy plane
above the sea in a world gone gray and savage,
in a marriage that battered me sideways
across dry dunes I could never have imagined,
until afterwards. My feet sank into sands
that shifted even as I pulled myself up the slope,
having left the crippled gull to harsh winds,
turning again and again, head on against himself.

We could not turn our backs to wind and sand;
the view was up ahead, a stretch of water,
a setting sun, out there, an unknown place,
a distant rise of trees, black against a sky,
a lingering light, some other place.
Maybe that was where the gull wanted to fly,
away, over there, to a place he did not know.
And now, I sit here, protected from the wind,
and place these broken images from a dream
that occurred just yesterday, back then,
a long time ago, the gull long dead,
on these scraps of paper from bits of memory.

But that was just yesterday. If we returned,
could we find the place, find the gull,
his bones, a bit of feather turning in the wind
a short while before tides erase all trace?
If we returned, we'd miss what lies about us now,
this stretch along the bay, these quiet waters,
this time when panic has disappeared, the plane
has settled, that marriage is just a lingering pain.
That poor gull has no existence beyond words
I pull together here, in his memory and our hope.
The sun is setting once again in a splendor of color;
we've found our way to the calmness of night.

CIRCLING TIGER

1

There's a stranger circling with a camera,
intensity across her face, no smile,
predatory handsomeness of a tiger
seen in a rare shot as she slips after prey
among outcroppings on some distant shore,
her eyes always there between bodies
she would drag to the dark of her cave.

While next to me, sitting mostly in silence,
is a friend who's had a major stroke
and will never work again, can barely talk,
can't read, has to be cared for constantly,
a pup with occasional bursts of memory
who comes to events where this tiger
roams and sniffs at vulnerable edges.

2

I don't know why I try to find words
for events I don't like, not that I don't
enjoy talking and stealing gestures like one
when an old be-hatted bitch bespotted me
in the crotch with a careless glass of red wine.
What a gesture to steal, as the tiger knows,
as we must know, to feed inner cavities.

Surely that's why we're here: to poke eyes
into eyes of those who wander, wounded
by failings of the world. She looks beyond
my shoulder and tries to remember names
and murmurs, "I must find something before
the tiger drags me." She had a brief moment
before snarling her way to a local diner.

3

But can one call them 'diners', when all
it takes is a one-room shack and a stove
and someone to carry beer? Disillusioned
women with eyes drained of tears, divorced
or addicted, will wait table, the most important
gesture; then all that's needed is one good dish
and wanderers will come to escape the tiger.

An active tiger may be why gay men party
in tight groups, as we sit and watch;
they're rough, tough, and trying to be pretty
with bright red or deep black hair in a rooster's
tail, underwear showing in a delicate band
of pink. One group circles warily
as a well-known Philly wasp gives a sting.

4

And over there, through dinner, elderly couples
with accents tell anglo-accented companions
about houses they've owned here or yonder.
The best place I've ever been — yonder —
the last place I hope to see again, up there
below a crescent moon... or down a crevasse
where a tiger roams with a flash of eyes.

Could it be that only a predatory tiger
or a mind with burning functions would know?
Could be; anything could be. This letter's
basic rhythm could be... could become
a poem, if the tiger will quit circling
with a threat to drag these aging fingers
from the keys — if I can just settle and watch.

LAST HORIZON

A ship on the horizon slips further away
each time I glance up from a scattering
of words across a page that looks a little
like scatterings of fishermen and swimmers
across a beach stretched in front of me.

Is that the ship I have expected for ages,
since storms began and I climbed to the roof
to see if I could tell how close the breakers
had come to driving swimmers ashore, leaving sand
deserted as if I could no longer find words

with which to build a shelter from devastation
of loneliness, the emptiness that comes
as storms continue and my ship slips away
and leaves whatever I might have wanted to say
in trailing memories of what has passed?

That's why I have to linger beside the sea,
close enough to find one day that the ship
is waiting at the door, the tide is high
and ready to withdraw and pull beyond
horizons marked by the falling of this line.

These are lines I've spent a lifetime building
even as horizons stretch beyond my eyes;
and we've almost lost ourselves trying to find
just where the intersections might lie for us:
there, we say, somewhere across the sand.

COMFORT

She pulls a shade across her eye
where there's no smile, no glint at all
as she closes herself against the world,
against a guy who tries to say
a word in comfort, a stroke of comfort
to ease his own disquietude.

Their lunch arrives and Dottie tries
to place some comfort beside the plate —
she even smiles as if she cheers
her aging dog, the one who seems
to have accepted death, who stares
without seeing that she is there.

"They recently married," Dottie says
and sighs and pours another coffee
and pats me on the arm and sighs
and turns away to pat the world
another way, a little comfort,
a little sauce to bring a smile.

It's a dying world wherever we are,
an aging waitress, a dying dog,
a bride who never learned to find
the world she may have dreamt about,
and questors who at least are looking,
though half blinded by the sun.

We look beyond the unsmiling bride,
beyond our tired and aging Dottie,
beyond a glare that falls at noon
with heavy heat and blinding light,
and know that we should go, put up
the shades, relieve the day with hugs.

LETTER POEMS FOR ISLANDERS

"Spirit is not in the I but between I and you."
                                    —*Buber*

I ~ SO MANY OF YOU COME AND GO...

So many of you come and go that I wonder
who's next; no, who was last and will be back;
young ones who wander restless across the world,
refusing to be codified: "We're on
our own," they say, as you have said, whenever
we ask where home will be next time, next year;
maybe, always maybe, you'll stop and visit,
stop and fill us in on vistas out there
where you find a brief love, a moment of joy.

I did it when young, much younger than you,
but worlds caught fire and pulled me home and left
memories of what was never seen; and Andrea
does it still, climbing Himalayas I dreamt of,
drifting down the Mekong, like one of you,
while I wait to hear echoes of her tales
in images she brings, in books that carry
stories I might have written and certainly devoured,
though now it's you, your story, that's what I want.

2 ~ I WISH, OF COURSE, THAT YOU HAD VISITED...

I wish, of course, that you had visited when not
so much was going on, fast trips to the doctor,
quick transcriptions to anxious daughters, and rains;
on the other hand, you saw us much as we really are,
under pressure, rushing to complete a project
because another waits just on the edge of anticipation,
and if not caught, will be forever lost.

Sometime, if we ever do it again, you must visit us
on Carriacou, Vieques, Cumberland or Delmarva,
where there is nothing to do except watch storms
approach and listen to an old fisherman quarrel
with a once-beautiful girl who's obviously trying
to break up for a younger guy not so likely
to be washed away in an approaching storm.

For a few weeks we read dozens of books, explore
local seafood, sleep long hours, and gather
those ideas, images, and possibilities on film
and slips of paper that may become a next book,
a next exhibition — certainly a few poems, a few prints
that would, if you were here, be tilted by your heart
and I could say "She was here when this was made."

3 ~ WELL, MY DEAR...

Well, my dear, since you now know you goofed,
I'll tell you, yes, you goofed. I got the second page
of a letter to someone else and thought a passel of things
about being sicker than you admitted. So why didn't
you say you were so sick? Or did you send this
deliberately but unconsciously, because it would reveal
much that you hesitate to say, consciously; and more...?

I'm glad to get it because it confirms a thing or two;
I'm glad to get it because I can use it in an encounter
with a dancer with little to say and a need to say more.
And what do you mean I'm probably not interested?
In what? The letter, the illness, or the drawing?
I care about all three. I want to see the drawing;
I want to send curative spirits your way.

Yes, I agree with the doctor who said you need
a month on an island in Maine. No, wait.
Maine's too cold. You need a month on an island
off the coast of Georgia or down here where water
is warm enough to swim each afternoon and sun,
oh yes, the sun is hot enough to warm those cobbled
parts of a heart we tend to keep hidden from others.

4 ~ MAY YOUR COMING TRIP...

May your coming trip among browsers be uneventful,
as were our days with you, only here for two nights
and gone, leaving calmness to linger where you
pushed among shelves of books, seeming not to mind
that, with us, there is little else to do until dinner.

Andrea goes off this week for a presentation
and book signing and lunch with friends from school,
while I remain to finish in comfort a casual book
by Morandi that caught my fancy and to clean
lingering remains of another snow storm.

Do you remember that beautifully hot day in Carriacou
when marchers in paper costumes strutted valiantly
through rutted streets, lead by Melda, glad finally
to be finished with night streets on the main island?
Boom boxes were deafening and we all cheered.

And did I tell you your friend came by for two hours
of wild tales and showed us pictures of her wedding
that were tolerable only because we saw familiar faces
in dark shadows, and wondered if that was you,
over there to the left, beneath the suspect Tintoretto?

5 ~ GOOD MORNING, MY DEAR...

Good morning, my dear, and it is: very bright,
very cold, and very still; not like the island
on which we met. First, thanks for the invitation;
but that's impossible: a dinner the other night
with friends close by took a day for recovery.
A price one pays for sensible old age.

Of course, it had been one of *those* weeks —
you've occasionally described them yourself —
last minute changes from the gallerist
and a snow storm on the morning of delivery;
and sudden word that we must go to press
without data from the Library of Congress.

By yesterday I had to take a Sunday off —
though, on general principle, I treat Sunday
like any other work day and never take it off.
I put on five CDs of Bach clavier music,
piled local and New York papers beside the chair,
took a dinner out to thaw, and settled for the day.

Of course the telephone started. Oh well...;
and, yes, a friend called to say she needed
a shoulder to cry on and came by for lunch
and a swim while snow piled high against windows
and we ended up laughing and finally agreed
that it was almost a better day without Bach.

She too had been an islander where we laughed
at snow like this; where we swam among barracuda
and, later, listened to Bach cellos, waiting to see
a green flash, that brief moment as the sun slips away
when a sudden flare of translucence may bring relief
to the heart and cheers from distant neighbors.

6 ~ SINCE YOU HAD TO LEAVE...

Since you had to leave the island, and it had to snow,
I hope you were there when it did snow,
as I know it did, though I can't remember when,
except it was about the time you were due back.

And since you did have to go back, or thought you did,
leaving us in the sun, I hope your trip completed itself
in a timely fashion and you didn't end in North Africa
because of storms in Italy that were, I read, unexpected.

Do you remember — come to think of it, didn't we
remember together while you were here? — that day
snow fell horizontally down The Grand Canal
as protesting workers released tens of thousands

of yellow balloons, which danced and played tag
down the Canal, coming to temporary pauses
in various water gates, drawing us out onto cold balconies
or into colder windows, which had to stay open

and draw out the heat? We cheered. We saw you.
You cheered. The workers cheered. Even the police
managed frigid smiles. And we never found out
whether the union got what it wanted or not.

Now, just because it's cold, there if not here, and just
because you're back to run things, doesn't mean
you can't keep in touch with us or with a recently
realighted boyfriend who challenges the regular one.

Look, when you live thousands of miles apart,
what happens when you are apart is irrelevant
to being occasionally together. Just don't sit them
at the same table; and enjoy your battered confusion.

Your most interesting words are "...certain habits
must change, new ones must be established."
I'm beginning to think that life is mostly a rhythm
of establishing and disestablishing habits that scar —
physical, emotional, or intellectual — a necessary clash
of cymbals that wake us and keep rhythms going,
if they are to keep going. Yours and mine do,
though there are times one might wish they didn't.

I dislike the word 'conversation' in the context
you've chosen even though it isn't misused.
Four laureates and an actress are hardly likely
to exchange and develop ideas in a free rhythm
of conversation, a spontaneous flow of ideas
that can leave surprised flights of dullness.
I would hope they'd be more prepared than that;
and they will; they wouldn't dare not to be.

I'm not out and about much, not even for close friends,
one of whom is at hospital today, having an operation,
where I should be, with words of comfort and hugs;
so most conversations have to be over the phone
or over lunch at a nearby diner. If it sounds awful,
it isn't; it's loosening — and bits of a limited world
become poems. Besides, we're still here where poetry
comes from the beat of the sea and small bars.

I'd like to see these people dig into something
like *Poetry and War* or *Poetry and Politics,* even *Politics
of Poetry.* Do you remember a passage in *The Iliad*
where everyone has started killing each other again?
All the heroes and gods are out there kicking shit,
and Homer says that Zeus looked down at all
this destruction and stupidity and laughed in bitterness,
just laughed, that's all he could do, laugh.

How long has it been since we sat over a bottle
and fought through a reading of Shakespeare?
You were upset that someone should think Lear's
"wheel of fire" a lust for Cordelia, that an academic
could not comprehend what Lear awakens to
when he mumbles, "I am a very foolish fond old man."
This from a man who earlier thought of himself
as an angry dragon. This old man, you said, tries
desperately to hold to something as his libido dies.
Males often do, as loyal Kent knows, sympathizing
deeply, knowing that Lear "but usurped his life."

Isn't the storm scene that has "drenched our steeples,
drowned the cocks" with thunder he begs
to "strike flat the thick rotundity o' th' world"...,
isn't this storm a realization of death to the libido?
There was a moment of silence as you and I,
not that much younger than Lear, thought about that.
"Here I stand your slave, a poor, infirm, weak,
and despised old man." And this is immediately
followed by that little nonsense song of the Fool:
"The codpiece that will house..." or, a little later on,
"This is a brave night to cool a courtesan."

Perhaps it is Freudian, and all the "o's" point there,
though even this seems to push it. You laughed.
Remember? What makes Shakespeare himself
is that he can give life to the pattern of a man's life,
and sometimes a woman's; that he can find words
to express our emotions, loves and hates;
that he can reach out, through actors, through print
and pinch away our intellectual pretensions.
Just a gentle push into the heart of human reality,
you said, as we all laughed and finished the wine
and wondered where the afternoon had gone.

9 ~ THE PROBLEM IS...

The problem is, one can never catch up with those
one is fond of and separated from. They, you, continue
to exist as part of a complexity that is I or Andrea;
a complexity that grows, becomes at times a mess.
So the complexity that is you or us has now changed.

You become something, someone, containing an old friend
but making a new one. After all, you've passed another 12%
of your life since we last met. Isn't that right? You are
about thirty (some 360 months) and it's been thirty months
since we saw you. Hmm? Am I trying to fill space, use time?

No. I haven't got time that couldn't easily be filled.
It's just more fun to imagine us sitting on Campo san Stefano
with an espresso or prosecco, talking rapidly through
a dozen topics before we go in different directions until
we pass tomorrow or the next day with an added detail.

Is that silly enough to say seriously that we miss you?
I hope so because it's been far too long since I've written
to play catch-up. For instance: How's the new house
from two years ago? And how's the young lawyer doing?
Is he still an active part of life? And what do you do now?

When biennale concluded, you sent a wonderful catch-up.
So have you thought any more about going to a museum
in the States? Have you checked for something at PGC?
Have you seen our favorite gallerist? She came out
for a couple of hours, while her husband painted a wannabe.

She talked a great deal about herself and a third gallery
she plans to open in the same small calle and people
who have insulted her by not speaking, and showed pictures
of parties where I looked for familiar faces in shadows.
And why is she so angry at the world or indifferent?

If you were here instead of in the silk and heels of Venice,
we'd bump you down a road, perhaps squash a mongoose,
reluctantly, and take you to a sea village where
there's no prosecco, but wine has been rechilled
after a month in the sun since it left your part of the world.

You might decide it's okay there are no paintings with labels,
no great rearing bronzes, and that a slab of chicken
plunked on greens is not so primitive after all. We'd slip
and slide through mangroves pretending we were headed
for an elegant drink at the Gritti while slapping bugs.

We'd spend a gritty afternoon figuring what thirty years
have amounted to. We do that, remember, to give focus
to the day, a brief day we have together, like back then,
an hour of laughter, a hint of tears, a charge of moments
with possibilities that may find their way to a life of words.

I was clearing up a pile, one of many in my office,
when I found a card with a splendid Delmarva painting
by Avery. Perhaps it came while we were away on Vieques;
perhaps I'm just making excuses. Perhaps I did respond.

Though I keep writing poetry every day, hundreds of pages
since *Dark Encounter*..., I do forget many things:
response lists, names and numbers. (Curiously enough,
though I can't remember music without the music,

I can play Beethoven sonatas I've never played before —
if, that is, I move straight through and don't try to know
what I'm playing.) So, if I didn't respond in a timely fashion,
I am doing so now, with profuse apologies — the best sort.

Had I mentioned that we have started going to Delmarva
for two weeks after Memorial Day, taking a house
on the bay, a house that looks out to the setting sun?
At least we've done it twice and will go back this September.

The painting on the card is beautiful whatever it depicts;
but, without being literal, it's evocative of a view
from a road over to the beach. In fact, I'd swear
that water bird was standing just there last September.

Congratulations on all of your accomplishments.
Do you remember Sarah, now sinking under twenty
Andalusians; she too used to be a painter.
Avery is better and might enjoy Andrea's website.

I wish I could say I'll be over for your next recital,
but I don't go out and about much. All energy is used
for writing. For goodness sakes, I'm an old coot now;
but I do hope you're still playing and still enjoying it.

Did I write this or did you? Did you say that,
in fact, you have returned to drink with bottles
upstairs and down, two bottles of gin, one
on the window that overlooks a gravestone,
the other at the kitchen door, on the deck.
Alcohol: instant gratification for foggy passions.
I believe that's what *you* said, since I can't drink.

And you bought a throw-away bottle to play with,
"to see pictures on my inner screen," you said?
(Actually, two bottles to satisfy a duplication disorder.)
More ginny passion, you said. Throw-away bottles,
whatever they are, are too complicated, at least at first;
"though I do need to slow down and keep some
semblance of sobriety, at the very least," you said.

And did you tell me that you, with some misgiving,
had returned to photography, with a Polaroid upstairs
at the window, overlooking the grave, and two downstairs
in the kitchen? "My photo passion," you said:
"Instant gratification and part of duplication disorder."
Did you actually buy two throw-away cameras
so you could follow what was happening on a screen?

"Those throwaway cameras are too complicated,"
you said, "at least at first try. I need to slow down
and keep some semblance of recording, at least
frame number and conditions of light." It sounds
as if liquor has poured out across the lens.
Are you sober now or simmering cameras
in a large pot of wine to serve over excuses?

...and then you said, "In the first stanza of part two
I wonder why you say *...in a chord this childish hand
could not then reach....* A mix of present with past
mixed me up. I wonder why you say *this childish hand.*"
Everything I was as a child is still buried within me,
though everything is different. Did I say that or you?
I can reach that chord today; with hands once small,
once too small to reach across unknown chords.

The poem is written these days in a present tense,
a persona, a mask, a speaking voice which is me
but isn't — just an old guy who looks back
over seventy years at things that happen in the past.
There's irony here, emphasized by the beats
of *could not then reach*: though now
in the present I can reach those chords, my hands
are stiff and find a child's flexibility enviable.

"But now let me tell you how I spoke it, beginning
the moment I sat down, in an unaccentuated breath,
the better to hear each word without special flavor."
Are these my words or yours? I'm not at all sure.
Do I remember correctly? Did I hear you say,
or did you hear me say there might be a third part?
I thought I was finished, until, redoing part one,
I found another and they gradually became one.

In writing music, there would be two movements
with structures that echo each other with differences;
each would have five sub-movements, and part one
would be more sequential in development,
while part two would be more like a set of variations.
I thought of Mahler while writing this. So, yes,
there could be a third movement, but only if it can repeat
those inner structures without being repetitive.

Come on, my friend; don't take all this too seriously;
now that I'm old enough to dismiss ambition
(a bit, anyway) I come to words improvisationally.
My biggest trouble has always been to let go,
a very hard thing to learn, but maybe I have,
maybe I've finally found a rhythm of my own,
a way to remind you of a favorite quotation
from Bach; you remember — I've often used it.

"You don't have to know where each repetition
comes in; but if I don't, then there will be a mess."
And Horowitz said: "There may be hundreds of notes
in a few seconds of this piece; but if I think of them
while performing, I'll not go there. The mind
can't work that fast; though in learning the piece
I had to play each note consciously. I had to teach
my body to think. It works faster than the mind."

13 ~ EVEN IF YOU DON'T SEE...

Even if you don't see this letter while you're away,
or in case you've carried your computer with you,
I wanted you to know that I just came up,
just read your dodging-the-bullet bit,
murmured a few curses (since there's no one
to speak aloud to), and sat down to respond.

Why? Curious, isn't it. Most of your explicit writing
has an abstract reader, not involving Buber's 'thou';
you've written for any of us who might enjoy
daily wanderings, something I can't do, but can admire.
And I haven't even seen you for over fifty years,
leaving us with a century of different experiences.

Actually, I woke at five this morning, two hours
earlier than usual, leapt out of bed and then staggered
to the pool for laps, something I thought I'd never do,
after an early fondness for a quotation by the editor
of *Great Books*, or someone, who said "Whenever
I have an urge to exercise I lie down until it passes."

At any rate, swimming back and forth on my back
(because I won't swim without glasses), watching
a pattern in the ceiling, long stretches of oiled wood,
I thought of people who have reentered my life,
after long stretches of separation, reentered my life
through long cave-like echoings of lost time.

And now, unlike you, I don't seem to have the stamina
to move much further than computer or piano,
or stove, with a rest between; but I do that, I hope,
with the energy I hear in your words, though
I miss that pianist whom even Beethoven, you say,
would have disliked, if he could have heard at all.

How I would love to go back... no, to move on —
to Aspen or Santa Fe, especially the latter, especially
if a Baroque opera were playing on stage, backdropped
by atomic hills. Had we made this reconnection
a few years ago we would have urged you over
to Venice and our guest room on The Grand Canal.

I don't mean this in any kind of draggy sense;
it's just to report that, even before getting your
Dodging the Bullet this morning, I was thinking of you
and picturing your companion and feeling good about
the little we share, even if I'd never be able or willing
to knock white balls into black holes across green turf.

Sometimes we just have to hold on. After exchanging
letters and hugs when you first shared news of needing
another operation and treatments in the city,
I crumbled a poem that wasn't working and threw it
across the room and started wondering what the hell
I could write to you in the way of warm verbal hugs.

That was almost two months ago and now I sit
here at my computer on the third floor and watch
the limbs of a tulip poplar resist heavy winds
that build, rougher each hour, with a hard drum roll
and dramatic flashes that may take the power,
and wonder why good people end with rough times....

I'm full of questions — about another operation,
about being away for treatment and visits with family —
which all boil down unsimply to how you are now,
how treatment goes, and a warm repetition
of an invitation for you to swing by at any time —
there's always an extra serving in the pot.

As I slide slowly into old age, resisting still
and still writing and playing the piano — actually
with another volume ready for press while admitting that,
with poetry, it does little good but still is fun —
Andrea is garnering kudos for new shows and books,
another due from the printer in just a week or so.

This success may complicate our trip down
to exchange hugs with you, which is supposed
to be as winter storms start here; but a local school

wants to do a retrospective of all her shows and books,
so Andrea will have to be there on several occasions:
it's the only way an artist can really say thank you.

That poor poplar tree just outside this window,
buffeted by winds, is a tough old granddaddy.
Several years ago, an arborist said he wouldn't make it
and should come down; we refused, but had to lop
his hollow top. Since then, he survives hurricanes
and blizzards, and, though a limb just fell, holds on tight.

Will we get down to see you while I can still let go?
Or will I continue to make excuses for hiding out
here on the upper floor of a long life where I hold
my own residue of words and their verbal sketches,
words I put together for someone else who may
be just as happy I've not appeared, just sent words?

We learn more about new friends in words we share,
in time we take to concentrate through time
on the other. You and I know so little of each other,
having only met two years ago, almost in passing
across an almost deserted terrace — and we've only shared
words and a hug or two on a hill above a distant sea.

You seem to hold on tight in a daily suspenseful fight;
you survive and share a tale of your companion, as I do
with you as with many of those I've met in far corners,
sitting at a café, walking on the edge of the harbor,
whispering to a friend in the dark hush of a bar.
We wander far and share across a cracking of the world.

Even though you used inappropriate terms
to which I had challenged you, and even though I was
so pleased I told myself to send a check right away,
it slipped around the edges of aging memory
as we went down to the island and, not having a you
to care for the place, fought the battle of making a home
on an island whose pace is slower than on your island.
Of course, that's why we're there; but we are there
for a couple of weeks while the plumber is off fishing
until afterwards. But we're fitting in, we left him cash
and a check is coming your way — at least it will
if I finish the possibilities of a poem in this letter.

Then suddenly I remember I've not sent you a copy
of *Lilith & the Blues*, which came out last month,
a serious omission since you fly around the moon
somewhere in the middle of the book, not a secret
since Lilith never really cared about secrets, which is why
those old men in the council were so afraid of her.
I think the greatest discovery I've made in my own life
is the discovery that hot dreams I had were for Lilith.
Oh sure, she often frightened me or, if not frightened,
made me slip to the back of the library where I dealt
quietly with my own madness — at least I never bought
the bailiwick of Eve, always suspicious of free apples.

Ah, my dear, there is one major disadvantage
to the wanderer's life we've led (which is the next book,
Gathering of Wanderers): there's always someone
high there in the Alps or in that little attic room in Paris,
or way out on the dunes of Cumberland where none of us
were supposed to be, or sleeping in a little shack
above Tom's Bay on Carriacou with homeless children —
and the relationship is intense, even if non-sexual,
for a week or a year, and then she flies away with a dragon
or I get carted off by mine. At least you write, when
occasionally you do write, quite eloquently (though Lilith
could do no more), as eloquently as I — so that helps.

EARLY MORNING CRISIS

We see them first as they come down the hill,
he wavering on a bicycle, she on foot,
lips tight to avoid a tear or angry cry.
We hear their voices only long enough
to catch a touch of New England leaking out.

He seems as old as friend Lee, a gray
pony tail, gray hat, beard even grayer;
and she a younger version of Arlene, large hat
and tense lips. And then we lose them, until
suddenly we see them in the middle of a road.

No cycle in sight, he cups her chin and tries
to pat her head as she ducks deeper
underneath her hat, pulls back and almost
stumbles to the gutter, never looking at him,
never looking up, just gritting her teeth.

He reaches to take her arm, to steady her;
but she ducks again and pulls away
and heads up the hill, while he continues to stand still,
watching her leave, and looks much older.
Then he turns and goes down, alone.

And that, we think, is it: we'll never know.
But not much later, we see them clutched
under a tamarind tree, old and crumbling
and utterly indifferent to whatever dispute
or reconciliation turns over an early morning.

SEARCHING FOR AN ANSWER

She pulls back and says she doesn't understand,
she never understands what the real point is,
not since we decided any answer is benign.

We'll have to get along without her help, she says;
the answer is somewhere else, perhaps over there
where shadows fall across a field in waves.

She's spent a life, she says, looking for an answer;
she's tried the wines in Italy and singular paths;
but all she wants now, she says, is a way out.

She often sits at the window and watches birds
or distant glitter of sun on a piece of sculpture,
a piece of polished steel under a willow.

Or she falls asleep without opening the book,
an old book she carries from chair to chair,
an important book she never seems to finish.

She only has a little time, she says,
to gain an understanding for which she's dreamed,
for which she's spent a lifetime's energy.

It's never there, she says; she's tried it all:
caught the last train out of town, followed tracks
across the snow — and it's never there.

"It's somewhere in these books," she says and points
at piles here or there. "It's somewhere here,"
she says and turns her back on the rest of us.

WATERS

Where would we be without water to escape across,
without water in which to drown or to dream that we
are out there floating over undesigned horizons
where we learned to masturbate in warm gulf waters
and foolishly assumed no one would notice, for there
were no neighbors that long ago, not at that lagoon,
not when I was still young enough to rub against
a beautiful body in a swift tide, though I know that in
a swift tide today, I'd probably sink and never rise?

And there were days in Venice when Andrea played
her flute in a window above rushing high waters
of The Grand Canal as an operatic soprano leaned across
the balcony of a palace just opposite and copied exercises
up, *do ré mi,* and down, *three two* and a repeated *one*,
until, suddenly, with a great splashing of oars,
a gondolier would pull to a stop in the middle of waters
where he would twist and turn and shout loudly
to both of them, "More melody; please, more melody."

And now, on our Caribbean island, there are rarely
any lights after the sun sinks beyond a distant horizon,
leaving a green flash; and each night we see a spread
of stars above dark waters, though we stop counting
as we pass a bright number to be stumbled over,
with a sight that can never make one feel stunted or lost:
it's too exhilarating, a large part of why we return
from distance to freedom from that limiting horizon,
freedom to believe that we might briefly take control.

MESCHUGGE

Our father, she says, would turn his back and snarl
'meschugge' when we tried to defend ourselves;
and some will say that much of what we create
when we are older and gonadally
still hot is little more than sweat from nonsense
that lingers in our head during restless nights
when madness of our father pushes us
into another world as mad as his,
but shaped by 'drafts of punch made from Lethe,'
as Freud has said with his own touch of meschugge.

No, she says; that's crazy thinking, she says.
The word describes a wandering in the wild,
forty years or a lifetime, so far from home
that we have no home to call our own, no place
to get our heads together, just horizons
that fall from sight, that well could drive us crazy.
It's not just Jewishness that we remember;
it's Odysseus spending all those years wandering,
not really trying to get home, or staying —
for home is a headache that drives him crazy.

You'll never understand, she says, that it's useless:
What our wandering is really all about
is a taoist virtue that just might help us see
those distant cliffs that overhang the past
and just might lead us on to a lovely spot
beside a lake where we can catch our breath
and maybe laugh in a coughing burst of nonsense
as we see how useless our wandering has been.
It's nonsense that will let the getting through
fill us with joy and a stir in our silly hearts.

ON THE EDGE AT LUNCH

In a long delay between watching a beautiful girl pass
through the room in a twist around clustered chairs,
and getting back to my desk and a yellow pad to make notes,
the details have changed: the girl was actually seated
at my table discussing directions sculpture might take
as someone interrupted to take orders for crab cake and beer.

The artist at the table, young and assured, could not know
the waitress was trying to support a son without a father,
as her every step came precariously close to a crevasse
that waits for all of us, any of us, the young artist herself,
in an unanticipated moment, a word from her doctor,
a slip of rope that holds her latest work high above the studio.

I can't remember which of the waitresses took our order —
unless it was the one who climbed from the crevasse again
last year and is just old enough to be the mother of the artist;
they are all beautiful girls as far as I am concerned, even
the heavy ones, for they care, they really seem to care,
even if on occasion, as when we ordered crab, the gravel slips.

The artist with me at the table seemed not to notice the drama;
or if she did, she was distracted by a double lifetime passed
since I was that age, with a mentor at a bar in Paris, trying
to pay attention, trying not to let my face disclose insecurity,
impatient with such an older world as his, when I wanted
to be on the river bank writing a poem in the margin of a book.

Well, drama's always on the edge, even when the girl
is beautiful and the beer is cold, even when I can't find room
in the notes for her young companion who is as bright as she,
even when I really didn't recognize the waitress at the table
that day, whenever it was we sat and talked of art and life,
wondering about paths that might avoid a slip to the edge.

LIPS THIN AND BLUE

For years, with lips thin and blue, she brought
our coffee, decaf and black, without asking,
pulled a sweater close and tried to smile,
sometimes eager to exchange a hug, sometimes
not even aware, after shoving mugs and turning,
that we were still there, still in need of omelets,
as if she feared we might see the bruised eye,
a chilled drip of sweat at the neck of her sweater.

We were told she had a boyfriend, one of the cooks
who scowled over hot splashes of oil, whose face
would appear at a serving window with a curt number;
and occasionally she mentioned grandchildren, one or two,
though she turned to another customer if asked how many.
She'd worked for the boss for thirty years, she said,
in a diner here or there, in small towns that shrank
and now on a highway where traffic heads away.

I asked if she too wanted to take off in another
direction, to get away; but she only frowned
and turned and told one of the boys to bring a tray
of mugs and make sure that they were clean.
And then this morning she seems to be waiting for us;
the coffee is poured, with extra napkins and water.
At first we don't notice, a moment of hesitation,
at which she flinches, until suddenly we see.

She's done her hair, short and neat, and no sweater;
she waits while we look and express surprise
and pleasure; and then she comes and gives us hugs;
and for a moment I think, I really think, she'll burst
with a story, something about her boyfriend, her family,
her leaving town; but all she does is hug us
and giggle and tell us she isn't on the counter;
and so we finish breakfast, puzzled, but with pleasure.

SOMEONE ELSE GONE

"It was only he, just he," she says
when she is sober; but when she's had
a drink or two, she'll tell about
the guy who came on afternoons
to whisper in her ear. "Real sweet,"
she says between a burp and tear.

The boys were born and then she ran
to Rome, to a poet without a dime,
who only lived a year or so
and left her to wander as she would.
Though she never found a boy to pay
her way, just got along, when young.

And after another life or two
she came back home and opened doors
for wandering boys just half her age.
And time goes on and begins to stumble,
though she stays thin and wears her skirts
split up the leg, revealing nothing.

I liked her then and now, for she keeps
a sense of humor wrapped in silk
and pats a wasted thigh and says,
"It always is the poet who dies,
just he. The others are distractions…."
And then she has to sell the house.

It's lonely in that part of town;
the house is dark; and most of the boys
are long since dead. Few can remember
her name; it's disappeared from gossip
until someone will say, "You know:
she wore her skirt split to the hip."

LARGE BAY

The surface of the bay shimmers this morning
like great hips of that woman the other night
who wore a glittering dress and no shoes
and fifty years that had not gone well,
that hung heavy with obvious indulgence.

That's just the way I've become these days:
I sit beside the sea and think of human
currents that place Odysseus, never
too anxious to get home, in a whirlpool,
and wonder if the warning sign's for me.

The sun is hot, the touch of water cold,
in a reality that prepares a metaphor
perhaps too easily, though the nice woman
with glittering hips might find it appropriate,
having known fever and chills of fifty years.

I sit beneath a mangrove bush and watch
a school of small fish reflect light.
It's only a beautiful bay carved from an island,
I tell myself. The water glitters in the sun.
It always has; it always will. That's all.

But of course it's not. There's so much more,
a world we make when palm trees rustle
and curtains stir with painful memories
and the sun disappears in a storm cloud —
and she reappears as a nurse in white.

WATCHING A PHOTOGRAPHER

She's on the malecon at the edge of a sea
that glitters a backdrop for colors she'll only wear
away from the grit of cities, out here or there
where sun holds off the dark and we sit
and watch strangers at a bar slip away;
and she wanders and lifts her camera to a torn face
while my notebook settles to record whatever
it is I think she may be looking for.

Sometimes a bit of that torn face she's seen
will reappear among words I've scribbled,
words that like pencils or cameras record
a bit of the world, the bit we see when we give
ourselves a chance to see and have the skills
to pull a knife against raw marble,
to pull resistant words or blurring images
from light, to pull back from easy use.

I watched her move among saints scarred
by tourists in Venetian churches and watch
her now, on a small island with messy harbor,
push hesitantly into a corner bar
as mid-day drinkers instantly go quiet
until a crowd of older guys, no saints
or tourists, decide she's probably okay
and invite her to focus for an hour or so.

And all the while ink scratches illegibly
across yellowing pages of a notebook,
my own sketchbook for the world I see or hear.
Then we retreat for work that might give life
to the lines you read, these very lines, written
perhaps many years ago while I sat in a jeep
to watch, to jot my notes, to keep an eye
on shadows from other directions, other dreams.

LIMBO

"Little did I know," she wrote in a brief message.
Of course she knew; she's always known;
though she might be lost in all the clutter
beyond time we've never known, not yet,
where distant calls become a muted echo.

She said, "Once written, the poem becomes
a part of the poet, the photograph a part
of the photographer...." Both become dust;
but with a little luck, poem and print
remain to remind others of what's possible.

"I'm sad to be awake so late," she emailed;
"it's part of grieving." With more grief than can
be known by grieving, we make marks
that come from grieving. If there were no grief,
would there be any remembering?

She said, "I feel I'm sitting in dust."
We all know it begins in dust, ends in dust.
This is why potters are ancient priests:
they transform dust into clay, into form;
with their hands they make it so.

Two forces stir the world, build or destroy,
often in the same jagged fall of lightning.
Water makes growth of beans possible;
water rises and destroys a hundred thousand people,
in moments. All dead. A hundred thousand.

Images and words are lives creatively fallen,
ignored or enjoyed, lived with richly, until they
and we are detritus washed beyond clouds
somewhere beyond time we've never known.
"How little we've known," she wrote at dawn.

DINER WORLD

Charlie moves and spreads smiles among the tables
and all the waitresses smile, even the cook comes out,
and for a moment tornadoes generated
by politicians, who would never eat in a diner, die
and I wait to see what drama will unfold.

Behind us, in a booth, a frantic woman tries
to sell a house, her car, herself;
while behind the bar our donna is pushing
her bank for a better mortgage, pausing
only to pour us fresh cups of coffee.

What happened, I wonder, to mornings
when, over eggs, I'd listen to horrors
of an ex-husband, the hope of a new one,
how lovely life had once been in West Virginia,
when we all knew it was nothing of the kind?

A carpenter, I think, perhaps retired,
but not a plumber who always has a wrinkled nose,
announces it is his birthday, one of many,
and all the waitresses sing "Happy Birthday,
Dear Charlie," and we send over an extra donut.

It's a brave new world at the local diner:
the cook had taught the seventh grade for years,
and perhaps given one hug too many;
and our anorexic donna wants to open a coffee shop,
with smoothies and a pile of poetry on each table.

"You could come and do a reading," she says.
She got a degree from Bucknell and spent a year
trying to do what her father said she should.
She's happier now, she says, and never wears a suit.
Even Charlie is something else I'll never know.

A FRIEND'S ESCAPE

"Somewhere he lingers," I say, lifting a drink;
"somewhere he wanders before the sun
filters through narrow streets.
If here, we'd've heard," I say, tippling.

"No," she says, "he's free at last. At least
we'll hear when wind has blown dust
from his hair and the murmur of Italian voices
has soothed his soul. Maybe then we'll hear."

"If there, we'd've heard," I say, sighing;
"our friends would have called from over there
to say they'd seen him slipping across the square."
"Not yet," she says, "not while he's full of regrets.

Give him time to smell salt in the air."
"But he'll not know he's missed," I say;
"he'll wonder if anyone can remember."
"No," she says, "don't worry, he's fine.

Give him time to find another route home."
"But what about news?" I say. "I could tell him
the garden is full of great phallic asparagus."
"Another time," she says, "wait for another time."

"I could make him grin," I say, "maybe chuckle,
a brief bit of laughter to follow tears."
"No," she says, "let him find he's free at last;
let him weep and find another way home."

RIDING A SILVER CAR

He rides a silver car as if it is a horse
and pauses while cresting a hill to wonder
if there could be one more adventure left,
another city, another girl to love,
to photograph, to imagine anything
might be, might lead him from a mourning stall
and set him on a trail away from heartache.

We never know what story he may have
on brief returns, a tale that differs daily,
a passionate involvement with a model
who's lost her way, a titled friend driven
by family quarrels, an exhibition in a gallery
where hunger is the motif of the owner
and circling wagons circumvent attack.

We call each other with excited whispers,
"Have you heard he's driven back to town?
Have you seen him yet? Will he come for lunch?
What happened to the girl with whom he swam,
he said, before they crossed the mountains?"
We're the ones with the curious twist
that envies him as he rides into the night.

SHORT PERIOD OF CLARITY

The day comes clear and, for a moment, calm;
surely today, I think, I'll hear the music we lost,
the rise of chords from minor to major,
that slight hesitation before rhythm returns.
It's almost calm in the face of a sea that, for days,
has filled our cup of tea with bitter salt.

"Shall we climb among the rocks?" she says,
stretching into sun that warms the terrace.
It wasn't possible before: Sun and dry rocks
were just a part of imagination until today.
We sigh and laugh but linger on the terrace
and reach out to let our fingers touch.

We've waited in a calm and casual way
as one does when younger years are gone.
And now the sky is clear, she arranges a still-life
and I make notes on another scrap of paper.
We come as close to singing as we can
until suddenly there's a bluster from the sea.

Clouds we thought had disappeared,
beyond mountains and surf we thought had settled,
are bringing darkness too early for distraction.
It's bound to be this way: You think a scar
is mended up there in the heart of the world
and look around and wonder where's the light.

THE WAY IT IS

She spends a part of each day ironing.
"Five shirts a day," she says and sighs and laughs;
"it's what I do." She breathes an account of what
she does to measure time, to move from dark
to light and spin the world in another direction.

She's done this for a while, she says,
and not because she ran away when the kids
were small and she knew she couldn't take it.
It was time to part and find her own way out,
across a world they never told her existed.

But that was all a few decades ago,
when she was young and the lovely poet
convinced her Paris was just the place for them;
and they went; and there he died; and she...?
Well, she was left to wonder if it was worth it.

Ah, she says she whispered to herself, I wonder
if I should go back home and do the laundry
and drive the kids to their music lessons
and tell him he's the best, the very best,
when he will know it's all a bowl of shit.

It seems he waited; and she... well, she wandered
through tsunamis of the world, and sang
for her supper in dark cabarets; and, well....
But that was long ago, she says, too long,
and she drifts into silences of memory.

So now she measures out the day with two shirts
before 10 and a soup like Aunt Tilly made,
and a clustered set of notes about the way
her life has twisted past the great iron gates
she thought were all a part of what it was.

The years accumulate, and the skeleton
is full of aches. "It's just the way it is,"
she whispers, over and over, "just the way it is....
Though it may make a story," she says, "a story
of the way it's got to be. It's got to be."

CALLIGRAPHY OF CLOUDS

On clouds that roll slowly from north to south
there are calligraphic marks, dark warnings
that grace a Zen master's scroll, a warning
that comes when it's too late to pay attention,
too late to send out words that might attract

loyal ones from distant mountains or that valley
where similar messages pull a group together
who vow to find a final image of hope
and vow that such a warning will stay alert
as afternoon storms blow down from mountains,

never again leaving us so radically exposed
to such final sweepings, leaving us charmed
by ways a brush can sweep that warning
across the sky and down through silk clouds,
in calligraphy of such intensity and peace.

AN ELDERLY PAIR

1

You'll see from the poem I send that I still work
right through stiffness and pain of plain old age
even as longer poems start, wander and quit,
like a set that featured the wanderingly wild.

One must let go as quickly as one must reach
to pluck a phrase that someone whispers softly
as a table breaks and we are strangers again,
each going on beyond the place we had.

I stretch into a world that may be spring,
for willows have gone from yellow to green,
maples have become red, and daffodils provide
a yellow carpet for the whole shebang.

So maybe now I'll start another series
as full of blossoms as those daffodils.

2

Of course I got your letter, not only readable
but mouth-wateringly ready to be read again
when hungry for lunch, a nice little set piece
to place beside a plate of carambola.

It will fit within a chapter you've already done.
I can see it now: a page of photographs,
two pages of commentary on the food you love,
and then an almost tearful account of his illness.

And then another photograph before
an angry account of a friend's presumptive laugh,
all this for a book that should be ready for press
just as you hit your monumental eightieth.

Think of the built-in promotional possibilities
with a dramatic death as you accept the prize.

OLD MEN AT THE BAR

Five men at the bar, old and worn,
laugh at their own forgetfulness,
and try to avoid for awhile the thought
of funerals, try to make them funny,
try to flirt with the attractive waitress,
and turn away when she responds,
turn away with a flush, avoiding eyes
of others at the bar, others like me,
as old if not older than they, who might
have been seen as a flirt if the waitress drank,
as at one time she did,
                              though now I watch
a clutch of five men at the counter who gather
twice a week in decreasing numbers and try
not to remember old friends who are gone,
old days when they worked together
on an office building at the bottom of the hill
or on the cluster of houses where they had lived
until their wives wandered away or died
and left them to meals at a local tavern
and dreams they seem to want to avoid,
dreams that fade to a hesitant burr.

GOOD WISHES

May this day be a day for painting well
no matter where the horizon line settles;
may bright sun lure you into wandering,
for a short while; and may a beautiful companion
smile and gesture
                    and make you sigh deeply
and think of the rareness of such beauty;
and may you shrug with delight and return
to pots of paint and another pair of canvases;
and may that companion at home smile too.

LAST NOTES

1

I'm not sure which was your 'last note'
or my last 'response' to a last note.
If your last note was yesterday, then
there's not been a response. Not yet.
But I can't find a note from you since,
I believe, last Saturday — or a year ago.

A rewording of one you sent a day before
expresses pleasure at a riff on painting,
as this is a riff on unidentified exchanges
that suggest a certain approach
to painting where no one, except the artist,
is sure what road gets us to a destination.

2

Destinations are always the passion
of painters.... (I really mean "artists",
but "passion of artists" doesn't sound
as passionate as "passion of painters" —
remembering that the problem with Dali
was a passion he had for blow jobs

that left his paintings ideational,
hooked up to the mind's eye.) Meanwhile,
to pick up where, somewhere, we left off,
a few times back, may I ask what response
you may expect to what you may have sent?
Has destination appeared on the horizon?

3

And now, backing up more than that,
getting to the beginnings of it all, what
had you sent to which no one responded?
Are you now asking if anyone got it?
Did it have to do with yellow trails
that leave darkness more than hinted at?

Was it about disappearance of cathedrals
in favor of steel mills or collapsed mines,
mere sign posts to deeper destinations?
These were responding messages, not notes,
verbal exchanges; and now I'm worried
about whether I got what you never sent.

4

Did those poems I sent days ago
say I'd be waiting for your response?
All I can say at this point is that, if I
could drink a glass of vodka these days,
I'd drink one now — a tall, chilled glass
full of not quite frozen vodka and ice.

Have one for me as you clarify exchanges,
though it's now been a longer time
than we might have thought — it always is;
and your paintings change, we all change
and throw exchanges out of focus from whatever
destinations there might have been.

A MIRROR'S WARNING

I

She's never known; she'd stare and feel the burr
that touched her neck and never know it was
a mirror to warn against dismissal, light
thrown back against all it was she feared —
an antidote if she'd but known. But no,
it wasn't even that, for now's too late,
the burr would say. "She's left with dotage, fear
and chills that follow from a sudden flash
that might have been in the corner of the eye,
or on the other side of a room where a cat
or something live waits in anticipation
of acknowledgement, a scratch behind the ear.
"It's nothing of the sort," she says aloud;
"I know myself too well for such a thing.

"It's somewhere else," she says; "It's something else."
And as the room closes down with fading hopes,
there's another touch of light that reaches
across space and crosses her heart, her skin,
with a lingering sense she has of hope and fear.
She rises and wanders through the dark and sniffs
aromas left in linens by her mother,
long now dead, but still denied, until
a box tips and drops the ancient comfort
that's hard to know, to acknowledge we are old
with a future that seems to twist toward the past.
And so we wake in the middle of the night
and feel that flicker at the neck, a light
falling from a high shelf across the room.

2

If we'd been out on the hill, we'd have said,
it's just a leaf, dancing across the snow
like an intoxicated rabbit moving
ahead of a small hawk. But who can follow
a leaf, even if it's the last from an oak
dry enough to move with a cold wind?
She'd be much happier with a different subject:
there are awarenesses she'd rather not face;
that's why she turns her back and will not look
to see what light reflects from the corner.
Even a leaf is something she says she's seen;
why see another, especially when the time
is running out and there is only time,
a little time, to bring it all together.

The mirror has a warning for all of us:
it tends to show the truth, unless we blur
the eyes with tears. She's not alone in this,
her hesitation to get up and see what's there.
It's easier to click these words at the screen
or transform images from this to that.
The *she* I wrote about last week is gone;
the *he* she painted not so long ago
was nothing really except a brief reflection
in the mirror we forget is standing there
on the other side of the door, waiting in the dark,
waiting to warn us what the truth might be.
So maybe we've never known and never will;
maybe we just need a scarf to hide the chill.

WATCHING FROM A LINE

1

I've spent a life scratching notes while I eat
and watch salesmen grumble — ordered my first brandy
in a bar on the overnight train to school,
and decades later wait for Andrea to return
from Buddhist temples in the Himalaya
while I eat a crab cake and drink decaffeinated coffee
and wonder, in words, why the good-looking waitress
seems mostly to live alone.
                  It used to be in margins
of a book of poems; but now I never sit here
without a small notebook and pen. Even when Andrea
is here, with her paper, I make a few notes
and we alert each other to a guy who'd crush another
in the john, who occupies a bench for two,
who never talks, even to the others at his table.

2

We talk, and I am interested in what she says,
but an aging blonde across the room, with hair
that swishes across a bowl of soup and a frown
that says she waits for comfort and some assurance,
distracts me — and I have to insist she glance
in that direction, though it interrupts
an important explanation she's unwinding.
"You wait," I say, "she'll end up in a poem."

Now here she is, trying to hide the years,
trying to find some comfort for all those years;
and she really isn't here, and Andrea's gone too,
and I'm propped at the screen, looking back
at the lunch we had, at the interruption I caused
by distracting her from a very good argument.

3

She clings to her mother's breast,
refusing to look at her father,
at least we think him that,
though the mother's sad demeanor
suggests a remembered past
before the child, before this man
who takes her where she doesn't want to go.

The child pulls herself tighter
against her mother and sobs.
It is a sob, we think, though buried
in the breast that had fed her; a sob
that only the mother can hear,
we imagine, as mother's arms clutch
and child murmurs, "I want to go home."

4

He struts among tables, a wrist
keeping time at his waist to unheard music,
and smiles to himself, indifferent to our need
for another coffee, even just a polite greeting;
he smiles as if remembering the night before,
a special night he might have said, with a friend
just back from treatment, anxious for company.

The smile is unconvincing, and finishes
with a tremor revealing more than age.
And, sure enough, a few days later we are back
and ask about the skinny kid who danced
and tried to keep his body moving
with possibilities for daylight. He's gone,
our waitress says, he simply disappeared.

5

To get his dog to shit, he leads him off,
over there, where we can still see him stoop
and strain; and for a moment I forget
my plate of monkfish, a soft and firm fillet.

He stands, pretending that he's waiting for
someone to show; he fingers his moustache
and restlessly turns his back on us,
sensing, I supposed, that....

No, it's not that. He's indifferent to what
people at a row of tables along windows
might think; he doesn't give a shit
what we might think of a dog that shits
in the fresh spring grass just below us,
just below where we sit with fish fillets.

6

We once invited her to see our gardens,
the fresh asparagus and tables of lettuce;
and she arrived with Italian cookies and questions,
wanting to know just which tomatoes bloomed
before the heat of summer drove her inside.

"I'm so glad I saw the garden," she says later,
in the slow hour before the restaurant closes,
during the hour we like to visit, the hour
when everything's in focus and there are moments
she'll pause at the table with a question and a smile.

"It's almost over," she says; "another hour."
I'm not sure if it's a sigh I hear, for she
can always smile, while serving table, and tries
to make lunch a pleasure for everyone.

7

I've sat here at the bar, alone, for ten minutes,
with an unused pen and not a scratch on my pad,
nothing until I decide I can't just watch the crowd,
can't just sniff irritating smoke of cigarettes;
I have to write something; I have to make use of time
before it weighs too heavily on my shoulders.

And so, you see, the first six lines have formed
a splash I hope to decipher when I get home
and light the screen; though actually, you see,
chili came and I stopped just where the 'splash'
occurred; so it should be obvious I was able to read
scratches in the first six lines and am almost here,
with a final eight, with a balance that keeps me going
until I reach a final closure....

8

I hope you're less confused than I and hear
the line that marches across the page, with drums
that occasionally miss the beat for what it is,
a thumping on the table as I wait for lunch
on a busy day when none of the servers has time
to pause and exchange a story, and Andrea's gone,
who'd usually be sitting right here to my right
trying to see which drama I follow today.

I watch from any place, and not just here;
though I have to tell you that as I gather words
he speaks with grace and looks me in the eye.
We've watched him grow, listened for his voice
to drop, and written of that; and now he smiles
and checks to make sure I have everything I need.

9

I have to tell her when she asks what I've
been writing for the years she's brought me lunch
that they are not about me, they're about
her or the aging lady in the corner,
the one who always dresses as if she'd just
arrived from a tea party or funeral.

She shrugs and lifts an eyebrow: "I've read the ones
on the website," she says; "you're always peering
through lines of words, scratching to get out;
you're there, I feel you there, as I know you're here,
waiting for squid and trying to hide your pen,
looking out at the room with a certain sadness."

And on occasion the room holds up a mirror,
and I'm astonished by something so familiar.

10

I'm not keen enough on ceremony, a wedding,
a funeral, a ritual of indifference,
that I would gather notes of instruction;
but civility, yes, I'd call for that,
for the syntax of a sentence, the smile and nod
when passing familiar faces as I enter
a bar, a diner, a small restaurant.

I took a friend to lunch and was chagrined
when he spoke abruptly to the woman who had,
I knew, just lost a child in another useless war.
She smiled, or tried, but been late with wine;
he carried impatience to a point of disdain.

I touched her hand for a moment as we left;
and with an effort she smiled as her eyes met mine.

AGING

I think the worst thing about aging
is the separation it brings between old friends
even when words still ring with the richness
of tower bells in Venice repeated on the hour.

See, I may not hear your voice
or see the crinkling slide of anger or fun
across the familiar pattern of your face,
but I wake at night to memories of you.

Memory is the load that takes a ship
to the bottom of the channel, from where,
sometime in the future, someone else
may pull out a clustered treasure.

I still hear bells and your voice
even as I settle between tides, laughing,
as I did this afternoon, at memories of you
as you squatted under a rise of Mayan steps.

Do you remember? Or was it the afternoon
we wandered through an old hermitage
dividing a shallow river that slides
through lower fields of Lombardy?

So long ago. It was all so long ago,
but I remember the effort you made to smile
in spite of whatever it was you felt,
whatever it was you had stumbled over.

MASTER OF CALMNESS

He's calm, he's quiet, he's always in control,
I think; he accepts the bumpy road, I think;
he's left skid marks on rainy afternoons
and we'd never know if he hadn't been seen
leaving the scene, returning to his computer
in a corner of the library where another set
of words waits for him to find the file
and pull them out in groups of rhythmic lines.

I've never even seen him hit the brakes
except, perhaps, the time she pushed him hard
and everyone saw her shake a fist and yell
a curse or two; and for a moment he stopped.
I remember that he sat behind the glass
for several minutes, and neighbors waited,
we all waited, but nothing happened, nothing;
and then he drove away, returning to words.

There's not a reference to that in the books,
which stay as calm as he, as if he'd thrown
a cloak across the muddy places in
his heart, a 'palliative' he might have said
and smiled, though no one asks him why his lips
grow thin with age, or why his fingers shake.
And then one day he simply ceases to be;
his telephone goes quiet, emails unanswered.

LAUGHTER, TEARS, AND SIGHS

1

Pretty girls turned away when asked to dance
and wandered across the room with a swish of skirts
and an echo of laughter at which I could only sigh.

And after the dance, when Miss Craig drove us home,
couples would pile in the back of her waddling car
and I'd climb in front and ask why Virgil was still assigned.

"Surely," I said, while trying to hear what was going on
in the back seat, "there's Latin poetry with a bit more power,"
something, I thought, about a guy left out by laughter.

Exclusion from such moments continued for years
of wandering, until I looked around and found pretty girls
dropping by the way in a panic of desertion.

Now I'm old and most of them are gone — and laughter
comes more easily as I sit and share my tale and regret
that I had wanted to laugh to put them down.

2

It took a long while to learn to let a tear drop;
there may have been a welling but no tear, nothing to mop;
it was not something, my father said, that a man did.

And now I'm old and it's still difficult. Oh, sure, a gasp
and dampness swells the eye when another friend dies
or sinks into arms of despair or forgetfulness.

But I no longer mind if another watches in surprise
as a tear runs down my cheek and drops on a letter
I grabbed to read while waiting for lunch at the diner.

The world has been too full of terror and horror,
not just what others have done but what we have done,
the dead we've left behind, the spread of hate and poison....

It's difficult for tears to balance laughter when
a bitter laugh so easily becomes a tear,
and tears will wash the world, wash it out and away.

3

She's old and limps and holds to the rail as she goes down
and glances, without a smile, at my fancy cane,
as I climb up, holding with a tremble to the other rail.

I sigh and nod, she sighs and nods, with no smile.
But there, was it a sound from her, from me?
She drops her eyes down steps to slippery stones.

I'm at the top, looking down, knowing right then
she'll become an image in a poem, at least a sketch
before the evening sun goes down, perhaps before

she's home again, safely, as I'll be when I write
whatever words will hold that moment, that sigh
when, in the eye of another, one hears one's own sigh.

She's dark and dour, ignored by an aging daughter
who rushes ahead, who doesn't see the fallen eye
or hear the sigh that's left for us to interchange.

4

A friend will read these lines and say, "I hear it now,
you've dug a trench and thrown yourself in muck.
That's why you smear mud across your sheets."

That's why I'd like to laugh or cry, at least one tear,
and push myself into a chair and sigh at what
climbs over the crest and drops into emptiness.

"An unresolved investment," that same friend says;
"it's what you gather to make another pile of words,"
and everyone sighs or laughs with bitterness.

I'll never know if I could have dropped a tear;
I'd like to say I did, but of course I didn't, not then
or now; except for anguish at another's pain, it's a laugh.

A soprano said on a Met broadcast the other afternoon
that it's all a matter of technique, not going mad,
but making an audience feel an echo of madness.

DOWN YELLOW TRAILS

1

When was it she left down a yellow trail
and left us floundering in the dark?
It didn't happen often, just once or twice,
enough to make us wish it wouldn't.

When was it I woke to find silence stretching
and dark tripping what might intrude, what might
take possibilities and crush them to dust
that settles on hope and lingers?

When was it she left, down what yellow trail
through heavy beating of nightmares
on her way to some deeper destination?
And where are the hopes that linger?

2

I begin to think that life is mostly rhythm
to establish and reestablish habits that scar,
a necessary clash of cymbals that wake us,
that keep the scar of rhythm going.

It's very dark and very cold and still
and I keep wondering where she wanders now,
down what yellow trail that leaves us in the dark,
when we could wish it wouldn't.

She's not a favorite bit of memory,
just a scar that lingers without healing;
and yellow trails are darker now than ever,
and I'm too old to really give a damn.

AT LOOSE IN THE WILD

1

It's not, he thinks, what he could have done;
it's not even the road he should have taken.
But how was he to know he could have, should
have said "No way, it's not for me"?
Not then, he says, not then at any rate;
perhaps never or not again, as he assumes
he must have said when he was young.
But it's what he did, in spite of everything:
He never said a word to anyone, not then,
not after he finds his way across the desert
and looks back to see a sand storm shift
as he pulls words together and strings them
in structures for another day, in acceptance
of a place where he has come to rest.

2

No, he doesn't see it, though he should have looked,
which used to be one of the things he always did —
he'd watch for red balloons, watch them slowly pass
and bring him closer to the rising moon, a large moon,
a great circle of greeting from distant mountains
to a world he knew which had no mountains,
just vast unempty stretches he was supposed to avoid,
especially when a red balloon would rise
and he'd wait to see if it would bump the moon;
but now he has forgotten that it is up to him,
that he is supposed to watch for what will happen;
but he was distracted by the heavy moon
and could not figure why it was only the moon
he saw, no red balloon, no confrontation in the sky.

3

It's always there, he says, on the other side
of the peak that pulls one's breath apart —
always has and always will, he has to assume,
even when he was young and the pause
at the crest wasn't needed except for a pause
to wonder which way down was best.
What's best, he wonders, when one path flows
like a stream from ledge to ledge with laughter
until he reaches the valley and the other path
takes him along an edge from where he can watch
the clarity of a distant view, there, way over there.
And now at the canyon's bottom, he looks up
with a shake of the head at how high that direction
even if sun lights the way with laughter.

4

On each wall hangs a smiling face with eyes
gone blank before a camera clicks to catch a face
that's wandered where sun will burn a perfect skin.
Now here they are in antiseptic rooms
where a doctor smiles and cuts an ear and jokes
that it'll not be needed any more: it's heard sad tales
too many times before. The blues play on the radio
as he lies and waits the doctor's cure;
a bulletin says a storm has hit the coast with many
drowned as these faces on the wall still smile.
They've seen it all, and then forgot,
as on a distant island they take their orders
to bring a beer, a plate of fried potatoes
and smiles, damn it — a tray of dying smiles.

5

He was fifty, he says, when he got divorced,
quit teaching, and set out to find what the music
of the world is all about; but after another 30 years
he says he's not found out, though he's had
a good time in exploration. It's what he says
has kept him going in one direction or another,
even when he searches among piles of words
still stored and funneled through his head,
though when he spills them out they drop as if
drawn to an end, though violins catch at the edge
and push the cellos to lend their strength to a shift
of rhythm as percussions roll and strike possibilities
of a dance, another song, another afternoon
with modulations that move beyond confusions of life.

6

"Not me," he says, "not again," and laughs and tries
to find a better inflection for the moment.
He pauses and looks about the room, and smiles
at tangible hints for another story — from a blonde
who used to be a redhead and married the cook
to a bartender who used to deliver babies.
"You'll see," he says and laughs again and turns
to leave the room with all he needs at the moment.
"That's all," he says; "that's all I need. For the moment."
We try to hear him out, to pay attention;
we whisper when he leaves; we turn and watch
as he pauses at the door, looks back
as if to say that's what he does, gathers a cluster
and piles them on a table in a corner of the room.

7

Will words work their way through mangrove
swamps where wounded manatees are caught
until a new sweep of tide gives an afternoon
for slipping through? Perhaps for Dante
the words were caught on a slippery façade,
for Yeats in a tangle of unresolved passion.
Did words ever come easily, a calm sail
across a protected bay with defined shores?
Perhaps it's what the user of words
has finally come to realize, that there are days
when muck pulls them in, and a phrase flounders
to the surface as if in panic, as if nothing is left
except a push, a pull for breath, for life,
for connections to give life to the sentence.

8

"That's what I do," he says, and twists about
as if his chair is pushing back unfairly.
"It's all I do," he says and pushes again
against the air he seems to fear, to resent,
at least to wish it not so intrusive, assertive.
His age has brought him to this stiller ground
on which one builds the last of what may come,
the laughter at what a day may bring,
the memories of lovely moments in the spring,
the friends who died and those who reappear
and share a tale or two of what the world
has turned around and shoved their way,
one last time his way as he rocks and says again,
"That's what I do; it's all I do." And smiles.

SMALL WORLD FULLY INHABITED

We never met when we were on the island,
when she was briefly there and gone again;
we never met in noisier surroundings.
We saw what she had done, two paintings, small,
in a corner of a room, that pulled us close
and closer, irresistibly, until Andrea whispered,
"She paints a small world fully inhabited."

We tried to buy them on the spot — after all,
this was an island gallery; but she
had left her mark on memory: "I couldn't,"
the owner said. "She painted them while here,
that very corner, before she knew a word
that I could understand; we spoke with touches."
They still hang in the corner where she painted.

We traced her down through islands of the earth
and cities where she had been, cities that had
the feel of islands full of wanderers;
and so we bought a piece or two here,
another there, to have a bit of her world,
a world that folds itself into a sphere,
a silver ball that sits alone in space.

Perhaps that's all we are and all she sees,
a sphere or cup that reflects windows, chairs,
an easel where someone may be sitting to paint,
looking out at those of us who peer
within and wonder if that's she, if that's
the woman we never met and know so well,
know sometimes better than we know ourselves.

RHYTHMS THAT ECHO

As long as I can find another word,
a phrase, a rhythm to echo the beating of
my pulse, a beating heart of some other guy,
a gesture that makes him human with hidden tears
behind an eye that's lost its gleam, its charm —
or the unexpected laugh from a serious face
that breaks with laughter of accepting age —
as long as this, another poem is possible.

Such poems may leak like broken pipes and leave
a mess to stain the edges of a day
before one even knows that pain is here;
sometimes they flow like melting glaciers along
a rock face and fill a gorge with pressure as ice
and water rise and words fill up the page
with running indication that there is still
a possibility of final catastrophe.

It's always me and someone else, seen
across a water glass at the diner, or seen
as she drops an anchor and stands back to feel
how well she's settled after a week at sea.
We meet through words tethered here on sheets
like sun-bleached sails; though I may never know
her name, nor she mine, we often nod
at a bar and talk briefly of taking up the anchor.

STARS RETURN

When suddenly there's a star I've not seen before,
or not seen for ages, just out there above the sea,
I shiver with pleasure as we do on islands that frighten
tourists, where at night the only lights are from stars
that stretch a path from south to north, horizon
to horizon, where, while watching bioluminescence,
so rare these days, we glance up and see a star travel
from here to there, sometimes remaining, sometimes
disappearing again, quickly and forever.

Even if one never sees such stars in urban skies,
I do remember, almost remember something
very special, funny or tragic, impressive or a little scary
with details that slip from memory. I've read
and liked those who soar too high, even if "liked"
is a stupid word and isn't what I mean, only
the beginning of meaning something; and I look
at pictures which don't ring a bell and think
the thoughts that there are crises day by day.

Only as I approach death are there fewer crises;
maybe because I now know there's nothing I can do
except keep writing, which for a while I do.
So it's never too early to find my own words
and forget a need to pay respect; that we write
is all we need, hoping words will rise like a cluster
of new stars, ones that return from time to time
in a flare above the horizon, above our heads
way out there where we were once afraid to go.

FINAL GOODBYES

I never like to say goodbye.
It's not that I'm afraid that's it,
there'll never be another time;
it's just a silence that will follow
the silence that was yesterday,
last year, those years it took mother
to die and every trip we'd say,
even when she couldn't hear,
goodbye, and wait to see if her breath
would stir the dust above the bed.

And now so many friends are gone
without a word that could imply
a goodbye that might have come close
to tears, unlike the open laughter
and hugs we used to share or shout
at close of summer when we left
for another life, a different rhythm.
"Goodbye," we'd shout as tires skidded
and for a while we'd dare not speak,
and even the children slipped to silence.

I have a friend who's near the end
and writes accounts of his last procedure,
and the guys with whom he shares a room;
the closest he comes to any sort
of goodbye is his description of the bed
that's rolled away before dawn breaks
and a new guy's brought in, silent
as if he's afraid he'll say goodbye
before he's even said hello.
He never signs his letters, just stops.

I did not know that as I got older I would write more than ever, that there would be little I enjoyed more than writing poems — as long as Andrea is close by, preparing photographs to share over breakfast, photographs like those in this book.

After *Dark Encounter in Mid Air* in 2004, I did little except brush Lilith and Xue Tao or wanderers I've loved into rhythmic piles of words, into songs and poems of an engaged old age. Soon there were too many for another single volume; besides, friends said, "We like thinner volumes than *Dark Encounter*"; and I actually do too, as with my earlier books.

So here we are, with the third volume in the last year, with maybe two more next year, and the next. New poems are regularly added; and old poems get refelt, rewritten, resung softly to myself as I stare at less and less messy manuscripts.

Early in the day, I read the paper and feel a need to write a poem in which Maureen Dowd sighs and spills her anger into prose; I go down the street to the local bar for lunch and watch Doc stumble in after another operation, perhaps, it's said, his last, and order a tall glass of vodka.

And as I read for an hour in the afternoon, I suddenly come across the Nag Hammadi version of Mary Magdalene and find that she's a Lilith, not the whore our religious fathers made of her.

By dinner, listening to music, finding structure for a sonata, hearing a vague cluster of words that evoke an evening in the cramped house of Bach, I leave manuscripts scattered across a desk or faded from the computer screen, and pause to make sure a notebook and pen are in my pocket while dinner simmers and a daughter telephones and I sigh with satisfaction and read a new poem aloud to Andrea and take an early turn to bed.

BOOKS OF POEMS BY HOLLIS

EARLY ENCOUNTERS

LETTERS AND VOICES FROM THE STEPPES

MIDLIFE ENCOUNTERS

SKETCHES FOR A MAYAN ODYSSEY

SCENES FROM AN OLD ALBUM

SONATA SONNETS

LAS ESPINAS

LETTER POEMS

VENETIAN VARIATIONS

DARK ENCOUNTER IN MID AIR

POEM-CHANTING TOWER

LILITH & THE BLUES

GATHERING OF WANDERERS

BOOKS OF PHOTOGRAPHS BY BALDECK

THE HEART OF HAITI

TALISMANIC

VENICE A PERSONAL VIEW

TOUCHING THE MEKONG

CLOSELY OBSERVED

PRESENCE PASSING

HIMALAYA: LAND OF THE SNOW LION

Design and production of this book were managed by
Veronica Miller & Associates, Haverford, Pennsylvania.
Production supervision was provided by Peter Philbin.
The book was printed by Brilliant Studio, Exton, Pennsylvania
and was bound by Hoster Book Bindery, Ivyland, Pennsylvania.